C. C. Georgeson

Report on the dairy Industry of Denmark

C. C. Georgeson

Report on the dairy Industry of Denmark

ISBN/EAN: 9783743340411

Manufactured in Europe, USA, Canada, Australia, Japa

Cover: Foto ©ninafisch / pixelio.de

Manufactured and distributed by brebook publishing software (www.brebook.com)

C. C. Georgeson

Report on the dairy Industry of Denmark

U. S. DEPARTMENT OF AGRICULTURE.
BUREAU OF ANIMAL INDUSTRY.
BULLETIN No. 5.

REPORT

ON THE

DAIRY INDUSTRY

OF

DENMARK

BY

Prof. C. C. GEORGESON.

PUBLISHED BY AUTHORITY OF THE SECRETARY OF AGRICULTURE.

WASHINGTON:
GOVERNMENT PRINTING OFFICE.
1893.

ILLUSTRATIONS.

	Page.
Fig. 1. Map of Denmark	9
2. Shallow milk tub	18
3. Setting milk in shallow iron pans	18
4. Setting milk in ice water	19
5. Cow of the red Danish breed	20
6. Bull of the red Danish breed	20
7. Cow of the Jutland breed	23
8. The Burmeister and Wains separator	26
9. Machinery connected with the separator	27
10. The Lawrence cooler	28
11. The Smith cooler	29
12. Prof. Fjord's control apparatus	30
13. Dipper	31
14. Pasteurizing apparatus	32
15. Danish churns	33
16. Butter trough	34
17. Cooling box for butter	34
18. Scrubbing brushes	35
19. Barrel in which butter is packed for market	49
20. Side view of cattle barn at Valdemar castle	67
21. Ground plan of cattle barn at Valdemar castle	67
22. Perspective of Madame Nielsen's buildings	73
23. Madame Nielsen's buildings—plan of basement	75
24. A typical coöperative creamery	109
25. Section of typical coöperative creamery	110
26. Ground plan of typical coöperative creamery	110
27. Arrangement of machinery in creamery	111
28. Projection of one side of Quist's creamery building	115
29. Vertical section from end of Quist's creamery building	118
30. Plan of Quist's creamery building	118
31. Ground plan and section of ice house	122
32. Use of ice in storeroom	124
33. Required shape and marking of oleomargarine packages	131

TABLE OF CONTENTS.

	Page.
Letter of transmittal	5
Letter of submittal	6
Introductory	7
Facts about Denmark	8
Situation	8
Area, soils, and climate	9
Temperature and rainfall	10
Condition of agriculture	10
Farm crops and their culture	11
Grain imports and exports	12
Size of the farms	13
Live-stock statistics	13
Annual output of Danish butter	13
Development of the dairy	15
Danish dairy cattle	19
The red dairy breed	20
The Jutland breed	22
Composition of Danish milk	24
Improvement of the cattle	24
Bull associations	24
Fairs	25
Official advisers	25
Dairy implements and machinery	25
Separators	25
Coolers	29
Prof. Fjord's control apparatus	30
Cream barrels	31
The pasteurizing apparatus	31
The churn	33
Butter-workers	33
Butter-coolers	34
Dairy scales	34
Buckets and milk cans	35
Cheese vats	35
Cleaning utensils	35
Systems of creaming	36
Setting milk in shallow vessels	36
Setting milk in iron pans	37
Setting milk in cold water	38
Setting milk in ice water	38
The separator system	40

	Page.
Treatment of the cream	40
Sterilization of the cream	40
Methods of fermentation	42
Natural souring	42
By the use of buttermilk	42
By the use of sour cream	43
By the use of skim milk	43
By the use of pure cultures	44
Churning	46
Treatment of the butter	47
Packing for market	49
Use of skim milk and buttermilk	50
Description of places visited	50
The Milk-supply Company of Copenhagen	51
Large dairy farms	56
Rosenfeldt farm	56
Aunó farm	60
Thurebylille farm	61
Valdemar castle	66
Faareveile farm	69
Julesberg farm	70
Brahetrolleborg	71
Small dairy farms	72
Farm of Madame Nielsen	73
Farm of P. Pedersen	80
Farm of Hans Hansen	81
Farm of Christian Rasmussen	82
Farm of Rasmus Andersen	83
Farm of Andersen Bros	84
Farm of P. Nielsen	85
Eskelund dairy farm	86
Ravndrop Vænzge farm	87
Holev farm	89
Hermans Minde farm	92
Dalum agricultural school	94
Coöperative creameries	95
Origin and growth	97
Organization—officers, salaries, etc	99
Kildevæld coöperative creamery	100
Constitution of Kildevæld creamery	102
Practical operations of Kildevæld creamery	105
A typical coöperative creamery	109
Renkolde coöperative creamery	111
Ringe coöperative creamery	112
Snóde and Stoelse coöperative creamery	113
Nonnebjerg Fælles creamery	115
Dairy bacteriology	119
Construction of ice houses	122
State aid to dairy industry	124
Markets for Danish dairy products	127
English imports of Danish butter	127
State aid to foreign markets	129
Instructions to Government Agent Faber	129
Restrictions on the sale of oleomargarine	130
Agricultural and dairy education	131

LETTER OF TRANSMITTAL.

U. S. DEPARTMENT OF AGRICULTURE,
BUREAU OF ANIMAL INDUSTRY,
Washington, D. C., September 6, 1893.

SIR: I have the honor to transmit herewith for publication the report of Prof. C. C. Georgeson upon his recent investigations of the dairy industry of Denmark.

Very respectfully,

D. E. SALMON,
Chief of Bureau of Animal Industry.

Hon. J. STERLING MORTON,
Secretary of Agriculture.

LETTER OF SUBMITTAL.

KANSAS STATE AGRICULTURAL COLLEGE,
Manhattan, Kansas, September 2, 1893.

SIR: I have the honor to submit herewith my report on the dairy industry of Denmark, which, under date of January 7, 1893, I was instructed to investigate under the auspices of your Bureau.

Very respectfully,

C. C. GEORGESON.

Dr. D. E. SALMON,
Chief of Bureau of Animal Industry.

REPORT ON THE DAIRY INDUSTRY OF DENMARK.

By C. C. GEORGESON.

INTRODUCTORY.

The facts hereinafter detailed were gathered during my recent visit to Denmark as a special agent of the U. S. Department of Agriculture. I was commissioned by Hon. J. M. Rusk, in January last, for a period of two months, afterwards extended by thirty days, making the time three months in all. I deem it but just to say that the short time at my disposal for the trip and the unfavorable season of the year when it was made—it being midwinter—prevented my investigation from being as thorough as it would have been under more favorable circumstances.

The following quotation from my instructions makes plain the object of my visit:

> I desire that your investigations should cover the three phases of the dairy industry, namely: First, the dairy farm, including the subject of breeds, yield per animal, feeding, general care, and the disposal and handling of the milk; second, the manufacture of dairy products, its methods and appliances; and third, the trade in dairy products, the value of butter and cheese in the home market and at ports of shipment, and other statistics showing the extent and distribution of dairy products and the various characteristics as to form, color, salting and packing, etc., required to meet the wants of foreign countries. You will proceed at once to Denmark to undertake this work and will complete it in the shortest time possible, returning directly to Washington (via London and Liverpool) to prepare and submit your report.

I arrived in Denmark on the 27th of January and left again on the 6th of March. The interval between these dates I spent in visiting representative creameries and dairy farms on three of the islands and on the peninsula, and I also made it a point to meet as many as possible of the men, both scientific and practical, who are identified with the development of the dairy industry. Among those to whom I am indebted for valuable information I would especially mention Prof. T. R. Segelcke and Prof. V. Storch, the former of the Royal Agricultural College at Copenhagen, and the latter of the Experimental Laboratory, same place; Konsulent B. Bóggild, Secretary of the Royal Agricultural

Society, also of Copenhagen; Konsulent J. N. Dall, of Fredericia; Konsulent A. Apple, of Aarhus, and Mr. E. A. Quist, of Skanderborg.

I am also indebted to a large number of dairy managers and farmers, some of whom will be mentioned hereafter, for information in regard to their individual methods in the dairy and on the farm.

I was everywhere courteously received. Although my presence on such a mission gave rise to a natural and freely expressed suspicion that perhaps the United States intended to compete with Denmark for favors in the English dairy market, this suspicion did not cause any secretiveness or unwillingness to give information. My many questions, which often concerned private business affairs, were in every instance answered cheerfully and satisfactorily. This much, by way of acknowledgment, is due to the many who, by their unstinted readiness to give information, met me more than half way and enabled me to collect the facts here presented.

The agricultural, and especially the dairy, literature of Denmark has been another rich source of information. I have perused no small number of publications of this character, first among which should be mentioned a work on the dairy by Bernhard Bóggild, entitled "Mælkeribruget i Danmark." The others are mostly pamphlets and reports issued by agricultural societies, and statistical works published by the Danish Government. Among the most important I may name the bulletins of the agricultural experiment station at Copenhagen, the reports of the official "Konsulenter" (advisers) in matters pertaining to dairy and stock-breeding, and publications by the Royal Danish Agricultural Society.

FACTS ABOUT DENMARK.

SITUATION.

A glance at the accompanying map (Fig. 1) shows that Denmark is almost entirely surrounded by water. It lies far to the north, being between 54° 30′ and 57° 30′ north latitude and between 8° and 12° 45′ east longitude. The climate belonging to this latitude is, however, materially modified by the large body of water surrounding the country, so that the extremes of temperature are really not so great there as they are on the adjoining continent, farther south. The map also shows the situation of the leading cities and the lines of railroad. The heavy double line across the neck of the peninsula is the German frontier. On the west coast, just above this line, will be noticed the port of Esbjerg. This port has sprung into importance during the last few years, and grown in population with phenomenal rapidity, solely because the establishment of a steamship line from this port to England has made it the port of shipment for nearly all the Danish butter going to that country.

AREA, SOILS, AND CLIMATE.

The area of Denmark is 14,553 English square miles, which is less than one-tenth the size of the State of California or about half the size of the State of Maine. The population, in round numbers, is 2,000,000 people, giving 137 persons to the square mile. The topographical features are not striking; there are no mountains at all in the country and the hills are not high. On the islands the land is generally undulating, with here and there a ridge of hills which range somewhat higher than the average. On the peninsula occur several long

FIG. 1.—Map of Denmark.

stretches of level ground, portions of which consist chiefly of drift sand and are overgrown with heather. These tracts are, of course, unsuited for agriculture. The soil is varied in character. In many places it is clayey and in others it is very sandy. This variation is due chiefly to glacial action, which is everywhere evident. The clay soil is, as a rule, fertile but difficult to work; the sandy soil, on the other hand, requires constant addition of fertilizers in order to produce paying crops. The climate is moist, although the rainfall is not excessive; but there are frequent storms of light misty rains which last sometimes for days, and fog and mist are very frequent, especially during the winter. The snowfall is variable, but, as a rule, the snow lies on the ground so as to furnish sleighing for two or three months each winter, and in some years much longer.

TEMPERATURE AND RAINFALL.

The average temperature for the three winter months ranges from 31.1° to 34.7° F; for the spring months, from 40.1° to 43.7°; for the summer months, from 57.2° to 61.7°; and for the fall months from 44.6° to 49.1°, the average for the whole year being from 43.7° to 47.3°.

The rainfall averages about as follows: For the winter months, 5 inches; for the spring months, 4 inches; for the summer months, 6.8 inches; and for the fall months, 8 inches. This seems to be a light rainfall, but it should be borne in mind that in that far northern latitude evaporation does not take place so rapidly as it does in nearly all parts of the United States, and hence a greater proportion of the rain can go to the direct benefit of the crops. Complete failure of crops on account of drought never occurs, and there is rarely a deficiency in the crops from lack of rainfall.

CONDITION OF AGRICULTURE.

Agriculture is prosperous, but its present condition has been reached only through a gradual improvement which began a century ago. At that time the peasants, the cultivators of the soil, owned but a very small proportion of the land they cultivated; it was nearly all in the hands of landlords. Since then the latter have gradually sold to the peasants a large proportion of the land, and now somewhat more than 50 per cent of the area under cultivation is owned by peasant farmers, and of the remaining land the greater portion is worked by them under a system of life tenancy by which the farm will sometimes remain in the same family for several generations, the contract being renewed by the son on the death of his father. A farmer, for example, desires to rent a farm which is tenantless. He agrees to pay so much in annual rent, in addition to which a certain sum is always paid down at the time the bargain is made. He begins to work the place, and continues to work it unmolested as long as he lives and his wife after him, if he dies before she does, but if she marries again the old contract is abrogated and a new one is made with the incoming farmer. This plan is the most satisfactory arrangement that can be made, next to ownership of the lands. The farmer feels that he is secure in reaping whatever benefits may accrue from his improvements. He can drain his land, or fence it, sub-soil it, and manure it without the fear that his rent will be increased or that he will be turned off and some one else will take the place.

A limited number of farms are rented from year to year, according as the parties concerned can agree. There are in the country quite a number of large farms ranging from 500 acres to 1,500 or upwards. These are, as a rule, owned by the families of the old-time landlords who in former days owned all of the surrounding country. They seldom work these large farms themselves, but rent them to tenants, who usually pay as high a rent as the farms warrant, leaving but a small margin for the farmer. He tries to widen this marginal profit by improved methods of culture and economic handling and sale of his crops. In these cases the lease usually lasts for a series of years, the number varying with the system of rotation in vogue, it being so arranged that the farmer can take one of each of the crops in the rotation from each field. Thus in an eight-year rotation the farm will be divided into eight fields and the lease run for eight years at so much per year.

FARM CROPS AND THEIR CULTURE.

To get a correct idea of the relation which dairying bears to general farming it will be desirable to look briefly into the character of the farm crops, and the relative proportion in which they are grown.

The following tables have been deduced from "Danmarks Statistik," fourth series, Litra C, No. 7, and show how the soil of the whole kingdom was in use on the 16th of July, 1888. What changes have taken place in the cropping since that time have been in the direction of enlarged areas in fodder crops. I have reduced the figures to acres in order to make the statements more intelligible to American readers:

Acres seeded in Denmark in 1888.

Kind of crop.	On the islands.		On the peninsula of Jutland.		Total area.	
	Acres.	Per cent of area seeded.	Acres.	Per cent of area seeded.	Acres.	Per cent of total area seeded.
Wheat	98,214	$6\frac{17}{20}$	18,760	$1\frac{1}{50}$	116,974	$3\frac{57}{100}$
Rye	239,130	$16\frac{7}{10}$	439,876	$23\frac{17}{20}$	679,006	$20\frac{18}{25}$
Barley	422,314	$29\frac{1}{2}$	298,119	$16\frac{1}{6}$	720,433	22
Oats	311,922	$21\frac{3}{4}$	718,269	$38\frac{19}{20}$	1,030,191	$31\frac{11}{25}$
Buckwheat	2,937	$0\frac{1}{5}$	51,823	$2\frac{4}{5}$	54,760	$1\frac{67}{100}$
Field peas	24,592	$1\frac{3}{4}$	7,457	$0\frac{2}{5}$	32,049	$0\frac{49}{50}$
Vetches	7,621	$0\frac{1}{2}$	1,633	$0\frac{2}{25}$	9,254	$0\frac{7}{25}$
Field beans	421	$0\frac{3}{100}$	33	$0\frac{1}{500}$	454	$0\frac{1}{100}$
Oats and barley mixed:						
For the grain	139,757	$9\frac{3}{4}$	85,128	$4\frac{3}{5}$	224,885	$6\frac{43}{50}$
For green fodder	67,154	$4\frac{7}{10}$	34,800	$1\frac{22}{25}$	101,954	$3\frac{11}{100}$
Potatoes	40,018	$2\frac{4}{5}$	86,304	$4\frac{17}{25}$	126,322	$3\frac{43}{50}$
Roots	71,005	5	56,876	$3\frac{2}{25}$	127,881	$3\frac{9}{10}$
Rape	794	$0\frac{1}{20}$	332	$0\frac{1}{50}$	1,126	$0\frac{1}{25}$
Miscellaneous	3,568	$0\frac{1}{4}$	1,921	$0\frac{1}{10}$	5,489	$0\frac{17}{100}$
Spurrey and lupines	3,265	$0\frac{1}{4}$	42,596	$2\frac{31}{100}$	45,861	$1\frac{2}{5}$
Total	1,432,712	....	1,843,927	....	3,276,639	....

Area in grass in 1888.

	On the islands.		On the peninsula.		Total area.	
	Acres.	Per cent of grass land.	Acres.	Per cent of grass land.	Acres.	Per cent of total.
Tame pastures	395,749	33 7/10	1,380,149	57 1/10	1,775,898	48 7/10
Clover and grass cut for hay	296,152	25 1/4	143,829	6 1/100	439,981	12 3/10
Clover and grass for seed	4,632	0 2/5	2,985	0 1/4	7,617	0 1/4
Fallow	224,721	19 1/4	249,527	10 1/3	474,248	13
Half fallow	84,572	7 1/4	66,372	2 3/4	150,944	4 1/4
Permanent meadow	120,610	10 1/4	433,892	18 1/4	554,502	15 1/4
Commons	49,108	4 1/4	114,868	4 3/4	163,976	6 7/10
Total	1,175,544		2,391,622		3,567,166	

Area in miscellaneous uses in 1888.

Gardens	39,148	4 1/10	29,221	1 1/10	68,369	3 1/10
Forest plantations	300,520	31 1/100	247,771	16 1/10	747,961	33 1/4
Marshes and peat bogs	500,116	51 1/4	242,264	15 1/4	292,380	12 4/5
Heath land	16,228	1 1/7	768,707	50	784,935	34 7/10
Drift sand	2,860	0 1/10	95,399	6 1/4	98,259	4 1/10
Stony land	12,924	1 1/4	43,357	7 1/4	56,281	2 1/4
Building sites	32,174	3 1/4	32,784	2 1/4	64,938	2 1/10
Fences, roads, and water courses	65,161	6 4/5	79,166	5 1/10	144,327	6 1/4
Total	969,131		1,538,649		2,257,450	

Referring to these tables it will be noticed that a very large proportion of these crops is designed for feed.

GRAIN IMPORTS AND EXPORTS.

As a matter of fact Denmark does not produce breadstuffs enough for the consumption of her own people. The statistics of imports and exports issued by the Government for the year 1891 show that the following quantities of grain were imported over and above the export of the same articles:

	Bushels.
Wheat	500,000
Rye	41,177,176
Oats	2,325,500
Buckwheat	102,745
Peas and beans	114,798
Indian corn	2,102,208

The figures have been summarized and reduced to bushels for ease of comprehension by American readers. The last item, Indian corn, is used chiefly for feed for live stock; as yet only a small amount of corn is used as food for the people.

This shows that a considerable quantity of grain is imported for home consumption and indirectly confirms the prominence which is given to the dairy. Barley is the only grain the export of which exceeds the import. The export of barley amounts to about 1,500,000 bushels; these figures, it should be noted, are not for any single year, but they represent the average of the years 1887, 1888, 1889, 1890, and 1891.

SIZE OF THE FARMS.

Graded according to their size, the farms of Denmark may be put into three classes, which we may designate respectively as large, medium, and small farms. The average size of the farms of each of these classes is difficult to ascertain because the statistics do not give the area of the land belonging to each class. They are classified upon the basis of taxation according to the quality of the land. The present basis, which is called "hartkorn," was established in 1844, when all the lands were revalued. But knowing the total area and the number of farms, it is easy enough to ascertain the average size of the Danish farms. Thus, in 1888, there were in the country 1,954 large farms. The size of these will range between 500 and 1,500 acres. There were 71,778 medium-sized farms, the areas of which range from 50 to 500 acres, and there were 150,260 small farms ranging in size from a small patch up to 50 acres. Now the total area of the country, excluding forests and waste land, and taking only what is under actual culture and in grass, is 6,843,805 acres, which makes the average size of the farm 30.55 acres.

LIVE-STOCK STATISTICS.

The latest available statistics I have on the subject are for 1888. In this year there were in Denmark 1,459,527 head of cattle, 375,533 head of horses, 1,225,196 head of sheep, and 770,785 head of swine. This gives 1.67 horses, 6.51 head of cattle, 3.44 head of swine, and 5.47 head of sheep for the average farm of 30.55 acres. It should be borne in mind that in estimating the average much land has been counted in which, for various reasons, does not support any live stock at all, such as gardens, and it also includes all of the very poor land and land fit only for pasture, and poor at that. In fact, it includes land of every description which has any agricultural value. At this same rate a 160-acre farm should support 8.7 head of horses, 34 head of cattle, 28.6 head of sheep, and 18 head of swine.

ANNUAL OUTPUT OF DANISH BUTTER.

The output of dairy products during recent years from this little country has been astonishingly large. Statistics published by the Government show that during 1891 Denmark exported 91,455,262 Danish pounds of butter, which amounts to 100,600,788 pounds avoirdupois. This is, however, inclusive of what was imported into the country and exported again. A considerable amount of foreign butter is imported and consumed there, presumably in order to save for export the more valuable Danish product. The total import of butter for 1891 amounted to 24,277,557 pounds avoirdupois. If we deduct the total imports from the total exports we get a surplus of 76,323,231 pounds avoirdupois as the product of the Danish creameries exported in 1891; but it appears from the statistics that of the total import of butter,

17,870,456 Danish pounds were destined for home consumption. Subtracting this from the total imports we have left 4,200,051 Danish pounds (4,620,056 pounds avoirdupois) of the import which was again exported. Now, if we subtract this small amount from the total export we shall get the actual amount of Danish-made butter which was put upon the foreign market in 1891, and this, it will be seen, amounts to 95,980,732 pounds avoirdupois. There are no statistics to throw light on the amount of butter which is annually consumed in the country, but it must be considerable. Bread and butter form an important part of the diet of the people. All through the spring and summer, from March to November, it is customary among the farmers and working classes to eat a lunch of bread and butter and cold meat or cheese in the middle of the forenoon, and another in the middle of the afternoon. And at the three regular meals of breakfast, dinner, and supper, bread and butter are, as a rule, also eaten freely. And this aside from what is used in cooking. In two cases in which I obtained data on this point I found that the family and help, in each case averaging about nine persons throughout the year, consumed annually at home about 660 pounds of butter. This would be an allowance of about 70 pounds to each person for the year, which seems high; but I believe it would not be too high an estimate if we should put the home consumption at 1.1 pounds per capita per week, or 55 pounds per year. The population may be reckoned at 2,000,000 in round numbers, though it is somewhat in excess of this (the census of 1890 puts the population at 2,172,205). The annual home consumption of butter would therefore amount to 110,000,000 pounds avoirdupois. On this estimate, as a basis, it is possible to approximate the total annual output of butter from the Danish dairies by a simple process of addition and subtraction. But first we should note that the consumption of oleomargarine is considerable, which, of course, goes to set free at least an equal amount of butter for export. The amount of oleomargarine imported in 1891 was 1,931,461 pounds, and the amount of same material produced at home 13,339,984 pounds; total, 15,271,445 pounds. The amount exported of this material was very slight—in round numbers, 500,000 pounds. This leaves a total of 16,248,589 pounds avoirdupois. The account stands as follows in pounds avoirdupois:

	Pounds avoirdupois.	
Estimated home consumption		110,000,000
Less total import of butter	24,277,557	
Less total consumption of oleomargarine	16,248,589	
		40,526,146
Danish-made butter consumed at home		69,473,854
Total export of butter		100,600,788
Total annual production		170,074,642

This is done in a country less than one-tenth the size of the State of California and but little more than one-sixth the size of the State of

Kansas. It is an interesting study and in line with the purposes of this report to consider how such results have been attained. An output so large would not be possible if it were not for a conjunction of favorable conditions, which makes Denmark a natural dairy country.

DEVELOPMENT OF THE DAIRY.

The growth of the dairy has been slow, and it is only recently that it has reached the present high standard. Some ninety or one hundred years ago the dairy was of little consequence except on the large farms; the smaller farms did well if they could keep the family in butter. It was not unfrequently the case that a farmer kept more horses than cattle, and the cattle received but poor treatment. They frequently had to seek their food from early spring until the snow fell, without any grain whatever, and when stabled in winter they were kept alive on straw and a little hay, the object being simply to winter them until they could again be turned to grass in the spring. Under these conditions they gave, of course, but little milk.

On the large farms the agriculture was, as a rule, farther advanced. The owners were well-to-do people of education who kept abreast of the times, and they generally employed competent superintendents for their farms. Their live stock was, therefore, of a better quality than that owned by the small farmers; still, there was but little interest shown in the dairy. Steer-feeding, on the other hand, was an important industry, and every farm raised and fattened for market a number of steers commensurate with the size of the farm. The Duchy of Holstein, which at that time belonged to Denmark, was the region where the dairy first developed, and somewhat later the island of Funen followed the same example. It was in these two districts that butter was first made for export and for the supply of the larger towns. The butter from Holstein held the first place and realized the best price in the market. Twelve cents a pound was at that time considered a fair price for butter.

The priests hold their parishes by the appointment of the Government, and to each country church a farm is attached for the support of the priest. These gentlemen were often the leaders not only in spiritual matters, but also in improved farming, and they, as a class, did their best to interest the farmers in the dairy and in the improvement of their live stock. Not a few of them have written instructive works on the subject. The political situation, in the beginning of this century, was unfavorable to the development of industries of any kind, but, as the troubles subsided, farming gradually improved, and it became more and more customary to employ skilled dairy women on the larger farms. These dairy people came from Holstein, and the methods they introduced were those practiced in their native districts. They had discovered that it was advantageous to keep the milk in a low, even temperature, and for this purpose cellars were built under the dairy-houses, and the milk was strained in shallow wooden tubs or buckets only 4 or 5 inches deep, and these were placed upon the cold stone floor for the cream to rise. However, the whole treatment of the milk left much to be desired, and it was only during the summer, while the pastures were good, that there was a surplus of butter produced. The cows calved in the spring, and nearly all of them were dry during the greater part of the winter.

The Royal Agricultural Society was organized in 1769, with the object of advancing agriculture by every possible means. In the year 1837 this society undertook to provide instruction in dairying for the young and promising daughters of farmers. It was exclusively a practical course and covered two years, which time they spent on one and sometimes on two or even three of the largest farms in the country where dairying was recognized as an important branch of the farming. They participated in all kinds of work in the dairy and thus learned the business from thorough, practical experience. Those who had thus qualified themselves had no difficulty in obtaining positions on similar farms, as head dairy maids, where they had complete charge of the milk and butter and cheese-making. Cheese-making, however, never became an important branch of industry. It was only now and then that any attempts were made to make sweet-milk cheese, and as to skim-milk cheese it had no sale outside of the country; this branch of the dairy was naturally confined to the manufacture of cheese for home consumption. Butter, on the other hand, gradually grew in importance. That which was produced on the larger farms was sent to Hamburg and Keil for export to England, and the poorer grades were sent to Norway.

In the beginning of the '50's many of the smaller farmers had begun to take an interest in the dairy, and the merchants who handled the products began to send their butter directly to England instead of sending it by way of Hamburg or Keil, as formerly. In 1854 the Royal Agricultural Society undertook, for the first time, to provide practical instruction for young men in the dairy business, as they had already provided for the young women. The object was, however, mainly to train herdsmen and feeders, who with this united the trade of a cooper, and made the tubs and buckets and other wooden utensils required in the dairies, particularly the barrels in which the butter was transported to market. This departure proved successful, and even to the present day the same class of employees is kept on the larger farms. In 1858 the Royal Agricultural School, at Copenhagen, was started as a branch of the already existing veterinary school, and thus gradually the number of skilled helpers on the farm was increased.

This gradual advancement received further impetus by the example set by a few of the most enlightened landowners. These were, as a rule, large property-holders who had been well educated. Etatsraad

A. Valentiner and Gehjmekonferensraad E. Tesdorpf are examples of this class of leaders. By the improvements these and others like them made upon their farms, they set worthy examples for others to follow. Much of the advancement was also due to the direct teaching of a few specialists, who, through their published articles, their lectures, and their investigations of scientific questions called attention to improved systems in the treatment of the dairy cattle and of the milk. The most prominent of the latter class is Prof. Thos. R. Segelcke, who has spent upwards of thirty years in continued work for the improvement of the dairy. He was first employed by the agricultural society as a public teacher in dairy matters, in which position he traveled all over the country, studied the various methods in use, both at home and abroad, and devised many and important improvements. In 1874 he was transferred to the agricultural school at Copenhagen as professor of Dairy Science, which important post he still fills. He had at first to encounter many difficulties in introducing the improvements he proposed. The knowledge of dairying, when he began work, was entirely empirical. The milk was kept cool because it was found by practice that it would thus remain sweet longer. The temperature of the cream in the churn was determined by feeling it with the finger, and salt was added to the butter not by weight but by guess. Prof. Segelcke began at once to alter these empirical methods by pointing out the reasons for the practices followed, and explaining how better results might be reached by following more exact methods. Having received a scientific training as chemist, he soon discovered that exact methods were necessary to produce uniform and satisfactory results.

He thus introduced the practice of weighing the milk that was delivered to the dairy, weighing the cream that was churned, and using the thermometer instead of trial by finger; and he particularly called attention to the advantage of keeping accounts with the cows, crediting them with the amount of milk furnished and charging them with the amount of feed and labor necessary to its production. He soon devised several forms of account which he published and which gradually came into general use, at least in the larger dairies. In traveling from place to place in the pursuit of this work he came into personal contact with all the leading farmers of the country, to whom he pointed out the methods by which they could improve their system, and he thus exercised a paramount influence on the development of the industry. Since his connection with the agricultural school he has, of course, been more confined and less able to take an active leadership in the practical dairy, but his influence has nevertheless been felt through upwards of a thousand pupils who have taken instruction under him at this school.

The system of straining the milk into shallow wooden tubs (Fig. 2), which originated in Holstein and gradually became adopted all over the country, after a time gave way to better methods, although on the smaller farms this plan is yet followed to some extent. These tubs are about 2 feet in diameter and 4 or 5 inches deep. They were sometimes painted both inside and out, and usually held together by two iron hoops. They were, in some instances, replaced by glass vessels which had obvious advantages in point of cleanliness, but they were too easily broken, and it was therefore too costly to maintain the necessary number in the dairy. Next, large shallow iron pans were introduced as vessels in which to set the milk. These pans were 6 to 8 feet long, from 2 to 3 feet wide, and about 4 inches deep. Fig. 3 gives a good illustration of these pans as they appear when in use. One end was made flaring, so that by tipping the pan the milk could easily run out, and they were frequently balanced on pivots in the center so that they could be easily tilted. This system of shallow setting was supposed to facilitate the rising of the cream,

FIG. 2.—Shallow milk tub.

FIG. 3.—Setting milk in shallow iron pans.

since the fat globules thus had but a short distance to traverse to reach the surface. These pans were skimmed by drawing the edge of a board slowly from one end to the other, thus pushing the layer of cream before it. This system is yet occasionally met with, although it is considered antiquated and unsuited to the most economical production of butter.

The next step in advance was the introduction of water in which to cool the milk. This, however, was not always practicable, as cold water of the necessary low temperature was, in places, difficult to obtain; but, the dairyman being convinced that a low temperature was essential to the best results, the plan of using ice instead of water was an easy step to take. Setting in ice water became common. For this purpose cement basins were built in the old milk cellars, and the milk was set in deep cylindrical cans which were sunk into the basins. This is still the method followed where the separator has not done away entirely with the setting of milk. Instead of cement basins, which were rather costly, ordinary large wooden tubs were often used to hold the ice water, as shown in Fig. 4.

It was in the beginning of the '70's that the idea of the separator began to take hold of inventors; but not until 1878 was the first Danish patent granted for a separator, and in the same year a machine was constructed, and exhibited in Copenhagen, which could discharge both cream and skim milk simultaneously with the introduction of whole milk, in a continuous stream. In 1879 it was improved and given the form which in the main it still has, and two years later, in 1881, the patent was bought by a firm who still manufacture it in yearly increasing quantities. The construction of separators had occupied other inventors. In Germany a firm had constructed a machine as early as 1877, but it could not run continuously nor could it remove the cream itself. It was necessary to stop and skim it and refill it with fresh milk.

FIG. 4.—Setting milk in ice water.

In 1879 another German firm constructed a machine which retained the cream and let the skim milk run out, and it was thus necessary to stop and empty it every time a given quantity of cream had accumulated. In the same year, 1879, the Swedish scientist, De Laval, perfected his first well-known separator, which was at once put in use in some of the eading Swedish dairies. Separators are now in general use all over the country. The "butter extractor" which, at one time, promised to revolutionize dairying, has never gained any foothold in Denmark.

DANISH DAIRY CATTLE.

There are, in Denmark, two distinct breeds of cattle besides a large number of nondescript animals which can not be referred to any breed. One of these breeds is found chiefly on the islands, and is known as the "Red Danish Cattle," the other is in the peninsula and is called the "Jutland Breed." Both breeds, or races, have been much improved during the last twenty or twenty-five years, but neither of them has, as yet, reached the highest limit of perfection.

THE RED DAIRY BREED.

The origin of this breed is not readily traced, but it doubtless takes its origin from a blending of the Angler breed of the Duchy of Holstein, which has been imported quite largely into the country, with the native cattle. There are other foreign races which, possibly, contribute, though in a slight degree, to the make-up of this breed. Thus,

FIG. 5.—Cow of the red Danish dairy breed.

Shorthorns have been imported from England, Ayrshires from Scotland, and some few animals have been brought from Switzerland. But the Angler breed has been the most important, and the present red breed also closely resembles the Angler cattle. As the name indicates, they are of a red color, the head is of medium size, horns small

FIG. 6.—Bull of the red Danish breed.

and curved inward, seldom symmetrical, neck light and short, rather depressed, shoulders fine, chest light, chine prominent, hips broad, bag large, milk veins very prominent, legs short and stout, weight about 1,000 to 1,100 pounds. The whole make-up of the cow is that of the ideal dairy animal. She is gentle and easily handled. Figs. 5 and 6 show, respectively, a cow and a bull which are representative animals of this breed. It is only during the last forty years that the farmers have awakened to the necessity of improving their dairy cattle. Previous to that time the dairy, as we have seen, was a subordinate branch of the agriculture of the country. At that time the farmers thought more of developing a beef breed than of rearing a race which should be superior at the pail; nor has the development been simultaneous in all parts of the islands. The start in improving cattle for the dairy was made by a few far-seeing men, and as their aims and objects became known, others have followed their example; but, even to-day, by no means all of the cattle on the islands can be dignified by a classification in this breed. Owing, moreover, to the division of the country into islands, which of necessity puts a barrier to the free intermixture of the cattle, we may find different types of the breed on the different islands. The Island of Funen contains the best specimens of the breed, and several herds which I there visited are unquestionably of high merit.

There are many examples of the gradual development of the milking qualities of the cattle simultaneously with the fixing of breed characteristics. Mr. Goldschmidt, in his treatise on The Development of the Cattle Interest in Denmark, has compiled statistics from several farms, which shows this development even in a brief period of time. Thus, in 1868, the average yield of butter per cow, on twenty-six farms, was 112.7 Danish pounds. In 1869 the average produce from these farms was 132.5 pounds, per cow. In 1871 the average yield from forty farms was 140.1 pounds, and in 1872 it was 146.4 pounds. Many other similar instances could readily be produced. The following table of milk yields in pounds avoirdupois from several farms and a large number of cows will, in a like manner, show a gradual increase in production:

Average yearly milk yield per cow in the herds of five farms named.

Year.	Sallerupgaard.		Rosenfeldt.		Oregaard.		Marienborg.		Egelykke.	
	No. of cows.	Average milk yield.	No. of cows.	Average milk yield.	No. of cows.	Average milk yield.	No. of cows.	Average milk yield.	No. of cows.	Average milk yield.
		Pounds.		*Pounds.*		*Pounds.*		*Pounds.*		*Pounds.*
1869	71	3,748			112	4,488	186	4,400	84	4,879
1870	70	4,167	166	4,523	114	4,400	200	4,380	95	4,472
1871	70	4,807	165	4,851	110	4,371	200	4,908	96	4,864
1872	67	4,887	167	4,639	115	4,409	220	4,192	96	4,785
1873	68	4,966	171	4,785	116	4,455	221	5,130	98	5,024
1874	66	4,561	170	4,589	116	4,532	226	5,187	108	4,626
1875	66	5,074	170	4,589	118	4,537	227	5,344	108	4,830
1876	66	5,489	170	4,449	121	4,466	234	5,193	111	5,121
1877	66	5,489	170	4,309	121	4,730	230	5,236	112	5,100
1878	66	4,922	205	4,404	125	4,834	231	4,937	114	4,473
1879	72	4,673	202	5,232	120	4,969	231	4,904	100	5,530
1880	72	4,141	206	4,698	132	4,535	225	4,991	109	4,684
1881	67	4,035	206	4,656	128	4,565	224	5,128	115	4,836
1882	61	4,988	202	5,542	125	4,679	232	5,042	107	4,892
1883	64	5,483	197	5,310	120	4,653	245	5,360	109	5,187
1884	60	4,947	200	5,459	122	5,205	249	5,336	114	5,434
1885	62	5,402			120	4,856	247	5,208	112	5,259

These yields are from common cattle of all ages and conditions. The table represents about the average of the Danish unimproved dairy cattle as we find them to-day on the ordinary farms. The improved red cattle are decidedly better, as shown in the following: On the farm named "Naesbyholm," on which in 1882 there were 89 cows, one milked between 11,000 and 12,000 pounds yearly, one between 10,000 and 11,000 pounds, two between 8,800 and 9,000 pounds, six'een reached 8,000 pounds, sixteen between 6,600 and 7,000 pounds, thirty between 5,500 and 6,000 pounds, and eighteen between 4,400 and 5,000 pounds avoirdupois. A farm on the island of Funen, which has for many years been noted for its excellent specimens of the red Danish dairy cattle, has given the following average per cow of five years old or more:

	Pounds per head.
In 1877	6,611
In 1878	6,970
In 1879	6,969
In 1880	7,933
In 1881	7,147
In 1882	7,365
In 1883	6,913
In 1884	8,292
In 1885	8,416

I have given the yields in avoirdupois. Some few individual cows of the breed will exceed these figures and rise to upwards of 13,000 pounds per year, but it would scarcely be fair to judge the breed as a whole by a few of the choicest specimens. Good average cows of the breed, with good care, may be expected to yield from 8,000 to 9,000 pounds avoirdupois yearly.

THE JUTLAND BREED.

The characteristic cattle in the peninsula of Jutland, which go by the above name, are black and white in color and the dairy qualities are not quite so well developed as those of the red cattle of the islands. They have been handled more as a beef breed, and, until comparatively recently, the fattening of steers was considered of more importance and more remunerative than the dairy business. The cattle had, therefore, for a long series of years been developed for beef rather than for milk. This is, however, now changed, and dairying is there, as elsewhere, the leading branch of farming. The origin of this race is unknown, as this class of cattle has been there from time immemorial. It may be said to be native to the soil and it has been only slightly modified by the introduction of foreign breeds. The color is not altogether uniform, but a large majority of them are black and white, much resembling the Holstein-Friesian breed. The head is usually black and the legs and tail white. In shape they are somewhat heavier in front than the red cattle, the dairy type being not quite so fully developed as in the latter, and the steers fatten readily and attain a good weight. The cows are a little smaller than those of the red cattle, especially in those regions where the soil is poor and the feed not abundant. They are distinguished for hardiness and thrive well on moderate feed. The milk yield is also somewhat less than that given for the red cattle. On many farms the average yield of all ages will not much exceed 3,500 pounds per year and on other farms the average reaches 4,500 pounds. This is for common, unimproved stock. In some exceptional cases, where special attention has been given to the selection of the herd, the average will go as high as 6,500 pounds, for cows in good condition. One of the best cows of the breed, which is shown in the accompanying illustration (Fig. 7) has, in the years 1886–'89 inclusive, given respectively 9,273 pounds, 10,488, 10,719, and 9,905 pounds avoirdupois; but this is an exceptional animal. On the farm where she belongs the average for the same years was 6,176, 6,799, 7,317, and 7,334 pounds per cow. One of the best herds of this breed is found on the farm named Borupgaard, in central Jutland. This herd has been so improved during the last twenty years that it is now one of the leading herds of that breed in

FIG. 7.—Cow of the Jutland breed.

the country. The improvement has been made by selecting the best cattle which could be found, regardless of cost, and breeding from these only. The milk yields of this herd, from 1880 to 1890, were as follows:

Year.	Number of cows.	Average yield.	Number of cows yielding over 6,000 pounds.
		Pounds.	
1880...	124	5,995	36
1881...	127	5,830	31
1882...	124	5,720	32
1883...	122	5,912	34
1884...	127	5,830	30
1885...	140	5,720	32
1886...	145	5,610	29
1887...	142	5,610	38
1888...	145	6,116	52
1889...	138	5,610	35
1890...	142	6,380	43

This average includes from 15 to 25 cows each year which were not at their best either by reason of having lost their calves or by reason of being barren.

COMPOSITION OF DANISH MILK.

In regard to the quality of the milk of the two breeds, the experiments of Prof. Fjord, in which the two breeds were kept on the same farm and treated in the same manner, indicated that if the Jutland breed gave somewhat less milk than the red breed, the per cent of fat was also a trifle higher, so that for the production of butter there was practically no difference between them, so far as this one experiment would indicate. The average composition of 43 samples of Danish milk, according to Prof. V. Storch, is as follows:

	Per cent.
Water	87.64
Solids	12.36
Total	100.00
Solids:	
Fat	3.46
Albuminoid substances	3.72
Milk sugar	4.42
Ash	0.76

This is, doubtless, a fair average of the composition of Danish milk generally.

IMPROVEMENT OF THE CATTLE.

As has been stated, the best specimens of these respective breeds are in the hands of a few breeders who have labored skillfully and perseveringly during the last two decades in order to improve their herds; but the general desire to improve has now spread all over the country and there is scarcely a farmer, be his farm large or small, who is not striving with might and main to improve his herd. This is shown in many ways. It has given rise to numerous associations among which, perhaps, the so-called "Bull associations" are the most important.

Bull associations.—These associations are made up of the farmers in a given neighborhood who unite and purchase a superior bull which they use in their respective herds. The purchase price is borne by the association and his keep is paid for out of the service fees. In many instances these associations are aided by small gifts from local farmers' clubs and from a state fund set apart for that purpose. I give an example which will suffice to illustrate all cases, and this is one of several which fell under my own observation. Such an association bull was stationed on a farm in the town of Ringe on the island of Funen. The association that owned him consisted of twenty-nine members, all farmers in the neighborhood. They had selected one hundred of their best cows and he was put to none but those chosen; inferior cows were not eligible. He was a good-sized, handsome animal of the red breed and weighed about 1,900 pounds avoirdupois. He cost about $162. The service fee paid by members was about 70 cents, but this fee fluctuates with the cost of his keep, as the members are charged only the actual cost. He was recorded in the herdbook for that breed, was 5 years old and had taken several prizes. The keep of this bull amounted last year to about $68, which sum was paid to the farmer who had him in charge, and one-third of this was covered by state aid.

Fairs.—The numerous district, county, and association fairs at which animals are exhibited and compete with each other for prizes have a wholesome influence on the improvement of the dairy cattle. Here the best types are shown, their good qualities are made prominent by the prizes they win, and purchases and transfers commonly also take place at these fairs. These institutions are helped, or maintained, under the auspices of the Royal Agricultural Society, which I shall have occasion to mention later. The fairs are a potent force in the improvement of the Danish dairy cattle.

Official advisers.—Another important aid, especially for the inexperienced breeders, is a class of officials who have become quite numerous. They are called "Konsulenter," from the word to consult, which, in a free translation, may be rendered "advisers." The state maintains three such officials in cattle-breeding, and three more for horses and sheep, each of whom is assigned to a given district. Many of the leading local societies have, in like manner, "Konsulenter" or "advisers" of their own. Altogether there are between twenty and thirty "advisers" of the latter class in the country at present. Their business is to answer questions and give advice on all knotty points which the farmer himself does not feel competent to decide upon. They are supposed to be expert in all questions pertaining to cattle-breeding. They are familiar with the history and breeding of all the herds and even individual animals in their respective districts, and, not infrequently, they are also veterinarians. It will be readily seen how they can render important service to the plain farmer in, for instance, the selection of a breeding bull, or in almost any proposed line of improvement. In addition to this they lecture at the gatherings of farmers in their respective districts, thus serving as public teachers, and in a hundred ways are of assistance in the improvement of the dairy stock. Under such methods it is apparent that rapid strides are being made in the development, not only of the dairy breeds, but of the dairy industry as a whole.

DAIRY IMPLEMENTS AND MACHINERY.

SEPARATORS.

First among the long list of machinery and utensils used in the Danish dairy should be placed the separator. There are several patterns in use, but the one most commonly used is the machine shown in the accompanying illustration (Fig. 8). It is there known as the Burmeister & Waine separator, after the manufacturers. The machine, which was invented by a Dane, P. Nielsen, was first used successfully in Copenhagen in 1878. It has since been improved and altered in many ways, but retains the essential original features. It can raise the skim milk and cream through its discharge pipes to a height of 8 feet, thereby enabling them to run off to other parts of the creamery where the reservoirs may be located. It is the only separator which can do this. Fig. 9 c shows this arrangement. It is manufactured in several sizes. The larger forms revolve with a speed of 2,800 revolutions a minute and the smaller form, which is designated as " *B* " by the manufacturers, revolves with a speed of 4,000 revolutions per minute.

Another separator, which I believe to be gaining favor in Denmark, is the so-called "Alpha" separator, invented by De Laval. I saw it in use in several places, and the superintendents invariably spoke highly of it. This form is peculiar in that it has a series of inverted tin pans in the drum, between which the milk must pass and which, it is claimed, facilitate the more complete separation of the cream. It is claimed that it can skim 1,750 pounds avoirdupois per hour, at a rate of speed

FIG. 8.—The Burmeister & Waine separator.

of 5,600 revolutions per minute, with the milk at a temperature of 75° to 80° F. The still larger form known as "Alpha 2" can skim, it is claimed, 3,500 pounds per hour at a speed of 5,600 revolutions per minute.

A third separator, which is used to a considerable extent, is also of Danish origin. It was invented and first brought into use in 1885 by M. Peterson and J. Nielson. They sold it, however, soon after to the present manufacturers, Koefoed & Hauberg, by whose name it is known. It is claimed for it that it skims the milk clean and works with comparatively light power. There are still one or two others in use of German origin, but only the three here named can be said to play any important part in the dairy business, and in point of numbers in use of each kind they rank about in the order here given. Each of these patterns can also be had in smaller machines for hand power, and these "Baby" separators are coming more and more into use in the smaller dairies.

Burmeister & Waine's hand separator is manufactured in two sizes, costing, respectively, about $68 and $95, and with respective capacities of 250 and 350 pounds of milk per hour. The Koefoed & Hauberg hand separator is also manufactured in two sizes, costing, respectively, about $154 and $117 and with respective capacities of 500 pounds and 400 pounds of milk per hour.

De Laval's hand separators are likewise in two forms, the "Baby" costing about $62, with a capacity of 120 pounds per hour, and the "Alpha

FIG. 9.—Machinery connected with the separator.

baby" which skims 250 pounds per hour. I did not learn the price at which it was sold.

We will next notice a few pieces of machinery directly connected with the separator. The receiving basin, into which the milk is poured after it has been received at the creamery and weighed, is sometimes a large wooden vessel, either square or circular in form, and in other places it is made of heavy tin. It is always placed on a platform so high above the floor where the separators stand that the milk can run by gravity into them. It is a well-known fact that the milk is skimmed cleanest when warmed to a temperature upwards of 75° F. The milk does not have this temperature when received from the dairy, nor can it be attained unless it is heated, and for this purpose a piece of machinery has been invented, through which the milk runs in a continuous stream on its way to the separator, and in passing is heated by steam to the required temperature. This machine is known as the "forewarmer" (see Fig. 9 a). It is a simple cylindrical barrel, made of tin or copper, which is "jacketed;" that is, placed inside another and a little larger vessel, so that a space is left between the two, and this space is made steam-tight. The steam is introduced into this space, and it thus warms

FIG. 10.—The Lawrence cooler.

the milk contained in the inner vessel. To warm it evenly an agitator is introduced, which revolves slowly, so as to bring all the milk into equal contact with the heated sides of the vessel. The milk enters the forewarmer at the bottom and runs out at the top. An opening in the discharge pipe permits of inserting the bulb of a thermometer so that the temperature can always be noted.

There are several devices which regulate the inflow of milk into the separator, or other vessels, so that the stream is constant from beginning to end, although there may be a variation in pressure. One of these is known as "Prof. Fjord's regulating funnel," having been invented by him. Another arrangement is to put a "swimmer" in the funnel. A "swimmer" is a cylinder with conical ends, into each of which is put a piece of wire, which thus forms the axis of the cylinder. One end, with its wire, projects into the discharge pipe of the funnel, and the other end, with its wire, projects into the discharge cock of the basin, or reservoir. Now, if the milk runs too fast, this "swimmer" rises up against the end of the discharge cock, partially closing it and thus regulating the flow. The "swimmer" is used in the funnels shown at gg, Fig. 9, and "Fjord's regulating funnel" at h. The cream from the separator is run into the suspended vessel d, from which it runs through the sterilizer e to the cooler f. The cream may run from the separator either directly to a cooling apparatus, or, as noted above, through a sterilizer to the cooler. We will note the latter first.

COOLERS.

Three forms of coolers were noticed, and all three cool the milk or cream upon the same principle. A stream of cold water enters the apparatus from below and running through a "worm," or a piece of thin zigzag pipe to the top of the apparatus, it is discharged, the end of the pipe being directed downwards and discharging the water below. The milk or cream is poured into a hopper on top of the apparatus and runs slowly in a thin sheet down over the corrugated sides,

FIG. 11.—The Smith cooler.

and coming thus into direct contact with the cool metal it is cooled to within 4 or 5 degrees of the temperature of the water used. The water may be supplied from a tank or large barrel placed so high that it will run through the cooler. Fig. 10 is a good illustration of the "Lawrence cooler," which I described in my preliminary report. The barrel should be filled with broken ice and a jet of water turned on to keep up the supply. From the barrel it runs into the bottom of the cooler, and following the zigzag pipe it runs out at the top and is discharged through a piece of hose. The substance to be cooled is poured into the small reservoir, whence it flows into the hopper, and then flows over the cooler. The Smith cooler (Fig. 11) is cylindrical in shape instead of flat. The water enters through the hose e and is discharged at f.

In some cases I found that the water running from the cooler was again raised to the reservoir by a pump worked by the engine that supplied the power for the establishment. This effected a saving of ice, and the water was cooler than it could be if drawn from some outside source. These coolers are made in many sizes. The largest is 3 feet, high in the body, and is claimed to cool 5,000 pounds of milk per hour, from 180° F. to about 3° F. above the temperature of the water used.

PROF. FJORD'S CONTROL APPARATUS.

This invention, which is illustrated in Fig. 12, is in universal use all over the country. It has, by successive steps, been improved and enlarged until it now has the form herewith represented. The Danes think a great deal of this piece of testing machinery, and are firm in the belief that there is nothing equal to it. The inventor is the highest authority in dairy matters that they recognize, and it is impossible that a thing he recommends could be inferior to anything else. I told them of our Babcock milk tester, but my representations met with no favor. The fact that chemicals were to be used in the Babcock test,

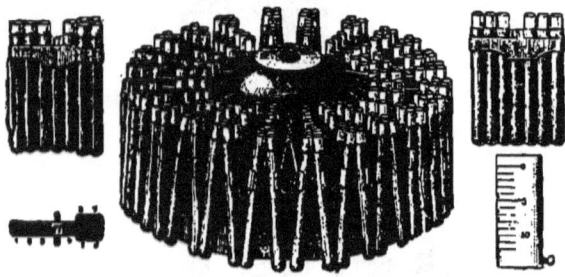

FIG. 12.—Prof. Fjord's control apparatus.

was considered an insuperable obstacle which might work dire disaster in the hands of common dairymen who have had no training in chemistry. Fjord's milk tester presented no such difficulty, and to them represented the acme of simplicity and accuracy. As shown in the illustration, it is a nest of glass tubes built up of twenty-four little frames which are suspended from as many arms radiating from a central hub. Each of the small frames holds eight tubes, the whole containing one hundred and ninety-two tubes, and being capable of making 192 tests at once. A small frame is shown both inside view and end view in the illustration. The tubes are about 6 inches long, and half an inch in diameter. It is essential that they should be of the same diameter throughout. In shape they are like the ordinary test tubes, except that the mouth is straight, not flaring. There are no scales or marks on these tubes, but the places they occupy in the frame are numbered from one to eight, and the frames are numbered from one to twenty-four. It will thus be seen that in testing a sample of milk it is only necessary to keep a record of the place it occupies in the nest. To fill the tubes they use a little dipper, represented in Fig. 13, made of tin. It has a little projecting arm on one side which is put into the tube after it is filled, and thus forces out a quantity of milk equal to the space it occupies. By this means it is possible to get exactly the same amount of milk in each tube. The test is on the centrifugal principle.

The Burmeister & Waine separator has a very large bowl and it is made to attach to an axis which stands perpendicular in the center of the bowl. The hub of the nest is put over this axis and when the bowl is set in motion the nest of samples turns with it, the frames being swung out so that the tubes occupy a horizontal position with the opening pointing inward. The cream in each sample is forced to the mouth of the tube, and by continuing to run the machine for forty-five minutes, which is the usual time, the cream forms a perfectly solid mass which fits like a cork over the milk. Now, by means of the little scales shown in the lower right-hand corner of the illustration (Fig. 12), this layer of cream is measured and recorded for each sample. Then, by reference to a table, constructed by Prof. Fjord to be used in this connection, the operator reads off the per cent of fat contained in each sample of milk. I was told by more than one chemist, who had compared the results of this milk-tester with chemical analysis of the milk, that when carefully handled it would work with perfect accuracy. It is not likely to meet with favor in this country; but I describe it because of the importance it has in Danish creameries.

FIG. 13. Dipper.

CREAM BARRELS.

The vessels in which the cream is set to ferment may next be mentioned. These were, in nearly every case that came under my observation, simple wooden barrels, although I learned that in some places were used large tin cans of a size suited to the size of the dairy. Sometimes only one or two were needed, while at other places I saw three or more in use. They were made of oak wood and each was supplied with a lid. A double cream barrel I learned was in use in some creameries. It consisted of a tin can fitted inside a wooden tub or barrel. The object aimed at was to maintain a uniform temperature in the cream by guarding against the effect of external fluctuations.

THE PASTEURIZING APPARATUS.

I described briefly this piece of dairying machinery in my preliminary report, and here present an illustration with a more detailed description (see Fig. 14). The form used in Denmark was invented by Prof. Fjord. He introduced an agitator to prevent the burning of the milk or cream. It is made of a copper cylinder covered with tin (Fig. 14*aa*).

This is fitted steam-tight into a vessel of somewhat larger diameter, *bb*, made either of copper or galvanized iron, and then covered on the outside with wood to retard cooling. The steam is introduced through the opening at *g* into the space between the two vessels and passes out through the pipe *dd*. The milk or cream enters through the pipe *c* into the bottom of the apparatus and it is discharged through the pipe *e*, which has a pocket on the upper side into which a thermometer can be inserted, thus enabling the operator to control the temperature, which he does by letting in more or less steam. The agitator *f* is a simple frame of wood or metal. It is turned at a speed of about 150 revolutions per minute by a belt connected with the shafting. This apparatus is in common use in Danish dairies. It is intended to kill the microbes, or at least the greater part of them, and thus prevent or retard their propagation, and it is used for sweet milk, for cream, or for skim milk, as the case may be. In some instances the sweet milk is sterilized instead of being merely warmed by the "forewarmer" before it runs into the separator. In other dairies I found that the cream was sterilized and again cooled at once before it was set into the cream barrels to await fermentation. And in nearly all cases where the sweet milk was not sterilized before it was separated I found that the skim milk was sterilized as it left the separator. This was especially the case in coöperative dairies, where nearly all the skim milk was taken back to the producers. Thus treated it would keep better, and in feeding it to calves it was claimed that all danger of possible infection with tuberculosis was avoided.

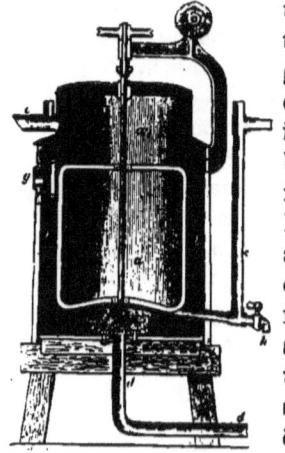

FIG. 14.—Pasteurizing apparatus.

The temperature to which the milk or cream was heated I found to vary somewhat, but it was usually somewhere between 160° and 180° F. It should be noted that in order to maintain this temperature constantly the steam should be admitted directly from the boiler. Waste steam, it has been found, does not answer the purpose. It may be noted in this connection that when the sweet milk is sterilized by being heated, say to 170° F., the separator can skim it much cleaner than when it runs through at a lower temperature; but, on the other hand, sterilization of either sweet milk or cream slightly diminishes the amount of butter. It increases the amount of butter fat retained in the buttermilk and it diminishes the amount of water in the butter.

THE CHURN.

The next important piece of dairy apparatus is the churn. Of this I found but one pattern and, I believe, only one size. Where one churn was not sufficient to do the work, several were used. The pattern used is represented in the accompanying illustration (Fig. 15). It is a large truncated barrel made of oak wood and suspended, as shown in the illustration, by pivots near the center of gravity, resting in upright posts. This arrangement facilitates the removal of butter and buttermilk and the cleaning of the churn, in that it can readily be tilted to any angle. The cream is churned by a revolving agitator made of wood, shown in the lower left-hand corner of the cut. Sometimes cleats are nailed on the inside of the churn to the number of three or four, which, by break-

FIG. 15.—Danish churns.

ing the rotary motion of the cream, assist in the agitation. In the majority of instances the power used is steam, but I saw also the churn worked by a horse, through the medium of a sweep. The illustration shows the butter-maker in the act of removing the butter with a sieve which drains off the buttermilk.

BUTTER-WORKERS.

The butter-workers used are of the same patterns which we find in this country; in fact, I believe they are of American origin. In former times, before the introduction of mechanical butter-workers, the butter was worked by hand altogether, in a trough, as shown in Fig. 16. It is simply a log of hard wood, usually beech wood, which is scooped out and made smooth. It is so placed that it inclines very slightly to one end, and thus the buttermilk as it is pressed out will run into a vessel placed underneath, through a hole in the trough. It is only in a few places, and where the dairying is conducted on a small scale, that the butter is worked by hand. The old-fashioned butter trough will soon be classed among the obsolete articles.

FIG. 16.—Butter trough.

BUTTER-COOLERS.

Butter-coolers are found in every dairy. The cooler is a simple box made either of wood or, in some cases, of zinc, in which the butter is kept to cool after it is removed from the butter-worker, and it remains there until it is time to give it the next working. The box is provided with one or more cleats inside, according to its depth, and slats are laid across the box on these cleats on which the butter is put, as shown in Fig. 17. In the illustration, *a* represents the cleat, *c* the slats, and *S* the butter. The box is covered with a lid on which is put a layer

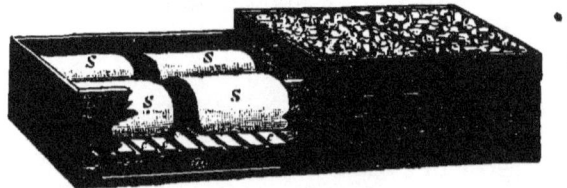

FIG. 17.—Cooling box for butter.

of broken ice, and the ice water from the melting of this ice runs down into the bottom of the box. To facilitate the cooling, the butter is rolled into an arch, as shown in the illustration. In some of the larger dairies which I visited these boxes admitted of placing two or three layers of butter to cool at once.

DAIRY SCALES.

Every dairy is supplied with several scales of varying sizes. The decimal weight is used everywhere. Instead of moving the weight along on the lever arm, as we usually do, there are two platforms, one on which to place the object to be weighed and on the other the weights of different sizes. In many dairies they use a weight on the receiving platform for the milk, which has a basin holding from 50 to 75 gallons. The milk is poured into this and when a certain weight is reached it is checked off and the basin is tipped so that it empties its contents into the large milk vat.

BUCKETS AND MILK CANS.

Of these many styles are used. They are generally made of heavy tin and they are not infrequently enormous in size. The cans in which the milk is transported are of two general forms, square and round, and the mouth is so large that it admits a hand and arm readily. Frequently the weight of the can is stamped upon it, or it is stamped upon a brass plate and soldered to the can, thus obviating the weighing of the can.

CHEESE VATS.

These are of two general forms, the oblong box and the cylindrical vat. In the latter the milk is warmed only through the bottom, which is double and made of copper, admitting steam to be injected between it and the real bottom of the vat. The square form is of the type in common use in this country. The cheese presses are also found in several patterns, none of which are superior to those in use in this country. The horizontal press is known as the "American" cheese press, and has been imported from this country.

Fig. 18.—Scrubbing brushes.

CLEANING UTENSILS.

Of these there is a large variety of scrubbers and brushes in use, some of which are represented in Fig. 18. Strainers, thermometers, measuring glasses, etc., are of numerous patterns, but I did not notice any that were improvements on those in use here.

SYSTEMS OF CREAMING.

The system now in use is, as has already been indicated, the separator system, but previous to its introduction there were, as noted under the heading of the development of the dairy, several transitions from one improved method to another, and all of these can yet be seen represented on Danish farms. I will, therefore, briefly describe them, inasmuch as conditions in this country may be such that a farmer now and then can use one or the other of them to advantage.

I.—SETTING MILK IN SHALLOW VESSELS.

It was early recognized that it was necessary to keep the milk in a uniformly cool temperature in order that the cream might rise in a reasonable time and the milk keep sweet, and to produce this condition it became customary to keep the milk in cellars or basements. These were not, as the word might imply, dark places deep in the ground, but they were usually 4 or 5 feet deeper than the surface of the ground, windows and ventilators to supply light and fresh air being put in; and to-day, with the improved separator system, we find these basements still in use, not because they are a recognized necessity, but because they remain in the buildings as remnants of a former system. In the new creameries, which are now being constructed, cellars are frequently wanting. The old method of setting the milk in shallow vessels where it stood from twenty-four to forty-eight hours before it was skimmed required an even, cool temperature, and the cellar was, in that day, the nearest approach to that condition. The milk was strained into shallow wooden tubs and these placed by companies and platoons in rows upon the floor, a narrow alley way separating one milking from another.

This system of setting the milk required an unusually large cellar. It required from 12 to 20 square feet of space for each cow in the dairy. This had the advantage that there was always a large volume of air in the room and that by careful ventilation the air could be kept sweet and fresh. It was also necessary that these cellars be thoroughly drained, so that all moisture which collected in the course of cleaning could be easily led off. The floor was usually made of brick set on edge; later on it was occasionally made of cement, and in exceptional cases it was made of hewn stone. The vessel most commonly in use, in which the milk was set, is shown in Fig. 2. The cream was skimmed off when it had stood, as stated, from twenty-four to forty-eight hours. In summer the skimming usually took place in twenty-four hours and in winter in thirty-six to forty-eight hours. This shallow tub was made of oak wood 2 feet in diameter and 5 inches high inside. The quantity of milk set in the tub differed with the different seasons, from $1\frac{1}{2}$ inches to about $3\frac{1}{2}$ inches deep. The chief objection to this system is that too much of the cream remains in the milk. In summer when it is necessary to skim the milk in twenty-four hours, frequently 1 per cent or more of the fat will remain and, of course, become lost to the buttermaker. The cream is skimmed off by means of a large flat spoon made sometimes of wood but usually of tin, circular in shape, some 6 to 10 inches in diameter and but little dished. The dairy maid would, with a dexterous move with this spoon, first loosen the cream from the sides of the tub and then gather it in rapidly in two or three spoonfuls and collect it in the cream bucket which she carried with her. The most difficult part of the management of this system is to know when to skim the milk, and to so ventilate the cellar that the cream and the butter receive no bad taste or smell. To get the best quality of butter the milk is skimmed while it is sweet. What butter fat is left in the milk is not to be considered as a total loss inasmuch as a large part of the skim milk is made into cheese, and what is thus lost in quantity of butter is gained in quality of cheese.

II.—SETTING MILK IN IRON PANS.

The long, shallow, iron pans which I have already mentioned (see Fig. 3), and which are yet seen in many dairies, were brought into use for the first time in 1843 by Hr. V. Destinon in Holstein. They are of several sizes, but perhaps the most common size is 7 feet long by 2 feet broad and 4 inches deep, having at one end a handle by which it can be raised and the other end flaring for the outlet of the milk and cream. Sometimes they are placed upon the edges of a brick basin, which is filled with cold water, the water, if possible, being made to circulate or run through the basin and reach to near the edge of the pan. The water is supposed to aid the cream in rising more rapidly and also in keeping the milk at a uniform temperature, but it has this disadvantage, that it keeps the air in the milk room very moist and more difficult to hold sweet and fresh, and in summer, when fresh air is most needed, it favors the formation of molds, which is decidedly undesirable. For these reasons water is not often introduced, nowadays, and instead of the basins the pans are most frequently placed on low stools or blocks of wood. These pans are somewhat easier to handle than the wooden tubs which, in a large dairy, are very numerous and of necessity have to be carried about from the milk cellar to the wash room, where they are boiled out and then cleaned in cold water; they are next placed in pyramids on racks out of doors to air and dry. The iron pans can be scrubbed down in scalding water without being required to be aërated and sun-dried in order to keep them sweet.

On the smaller farms, where the dairy consists of only a few cows, the milk has very generally been set either in earthenware dishes or in enameled iron pans. These are still in common use on small farms, and they are placed either on the floor or on shelves in the milk room. The chief objection to all of these forms of setting the milk lies usually in the premises. If it is possible to have a dry cellar on the north side of the house, so situated that no bad odors from outside can get into it with any direction of the wind and which permits free ventilation, this system of setting milk, especially when the skim milk is used for cheese, is not a bad one. But in too many cases it is difficult to meet these necessary conditions, and whenever the cellar is objectionable it is impossible to make a first-class article of butter.

III.—SETTING MILK IN COLD WATER.

This system, which was used in some dairies for a number of years, was borrowed from America, and it was even sometimes called the "Orange County System," after Orange County, N. Y., where it was common. The plan consisted, as in this country, of setting the milk in deep cans in cold water—spring water, if it could be obtained; well water raised by a pump, if nothing better could be had. However, it never came into general use, although the results were, on the whole, satisfactory where the water supply was sufficient. Some of the leading farmers adopted the plan, but after some years it was modified by the use of ice.

IV.—SETTING MILK IN ICE WATER.

The use of ice was the outgrowth of the cold-water method. A few trials proved conclusively the great advantage of cooling the milk rapidly and maintaining it at the lowest possible temperature by the use of ice. But the great difficulty was to preserve a sufficient quantity of ice for this use in a large dairy. This question led to Prof. Fjord's experiments in the construction of ice houses, which I shall mention later on. Early in the '70's the practice of using ice to cool the milk became general wherever it was practicable to obtain and store the ice. The method was to use the old water basins constructed some eight or ten years before, when the water system came into repute. The conditions were favorable to the use of ice; that is, the aim had been all along in the construction of milk cellars to reduce the temperature to the minimum in warm weather, so that the ice lasted longer than it would have done had the milk room been entirely above ground and no provision made for the use of cold water. On the smaller farms the ice basin frequently consisted of large wooden tubs of the proper depth, into which the cans were sunk (see Fig. 4). I found this method in use yet on many of the smaller places where the milk was not sold soon after milking to some neighboring creamery, or where the separator had not been introduced. Prof. Fjord, who has done so much for the development of the Danish dairy, experimented largely in order to ascertain the relative values of setting milk in cold water and in ice water. By cold water we are to understand such water as can be obtained from springs and wells, usually in that country ranging in temperature between 50° and 60° Fahrenheit. He proved conclusively that the milk ought to be cooled as soon as possible to a temperature as near freezing as could be obtained, by the use of ice water in summer; and he proved further that the depth of the milk in the can had but little influence on the rapidity of the rising of the cream, provided it was kept at a low temperature.

The following table, by Prof. Fjord, shows the advantage of rapid cooling to a low temperature compared with the use of cold, still water:

	Cream from milk skimmed after standing ten hours.			Cream from milk skimmed after standing thirty-four hours.		
	In ice cooled at 35° to 36° F.	In still water at—		In ice cooled at 35° to 36° F.	In still water at—	
		39° to 40° F.	50° F.		39° to 40° F.	50° F.
	Per cent.	Per cent.	Per cent.	Per cent.	Per cent.	Per cent.
Average of experiment	100	96.4	74.9	100	98.6	86.6
Per cent of cream lost by use of water without ice		3.6	25.1		1.4	13.4

From this it will be seen that a great loss is sustained by setting the milk even at so low a temperature as 50°, compared with a temperature but little above freezing. The next table shows the loss in per cent of butter, which is sustained by skimming the milk after standing ten hours, compared with thirty-four hours' standing, both by the use of ice and the use of water at different temperatures.

	Per cent of butter by standing.		Loss of butter in per cent by standing.	
	Thirty-four hours.	Ten hours.	Thirty-four hours.	Ten hours.
Perfect cooling in ice	100	94.3	0.	5.7
Imperfect cooling in ice		90.3		9.7
Cooling in water at—				
39.2° F	98.6	90.9	1.4	9.1
42.8° F	96.8		3.2	
46.4° F	91.9	80.7	8.1	19.3
50° F	87.0	70.6	13.0	29.4
51.8° F	85.5	70.1	14.5	29.9
53.6° F	83.6		16.4	

These results were obtained by Prof. Fjord in his experiments on the subject. The table is copied from "Mælkeribruget i Danmark," by B. Bóggild.

Prof. Fjord also constructed tables showing the amount of ice required to cool 100 pounds of milk under different conditions, during the several months of the year. The experiment, however, was based upon the average temperature of each month in Denmark. As the conditions in America vary greatly in different places, all of which will have a higher average temperature in summer than there is in Denmark, these tables will not have much practical value for us. By the use of good ice houses and by careful, economical use of the ice, the safest guide to follow will be to put up as much ice as the weight of the milk which is to be handled throughout the year, pound for pound.

V.—THE SEPARATOR SYSTEM.

As already stated, the separator is now in general use. It will not be necessary to detail the method of operation followed, inasmuch as it is known to every creamery man in this country. I will note only a point or two which are not generally practiced here. I have already called attention to the Burmeister & Waine separator, by means of which the cream and milk can be transported through pipes to their respective reservoirs directly from the separator (see Fig. 9). In the coöperative creameries it is now a common practice to sterilize the skim milk directly after it leaves the separator, and wherever this make of the separator is used the skim milk is carried to the sterilizer, often at an elevation of 6 or more feet above the separator, without the intervention of pump or any other force than that given to it by the drum in the separator. The cream is in like manner carried to the cream barrel, if so desired. This is a saving of labor which is not possible with any other separator. The one objection which I found urged against this method of transmitting milk and cream was that it frothed too much. The skim milk is sterilized at a temperature very near the boiling point when it is not intended to use it for cheese. The object is twofold—first, to increase its keeping qualities so that it can be carried back to the farms without souring, and, second, it is sterilized in order to kill possible germs of contagion, such as tuberculosis. The milk coming in from so many places there is always a strong presumption that some of the cows may be tuberculous, although they may not show it by examination; and the milk being mixed, other dairy farmers with sound cattle object to using the milk in their households and for their calves and pigs unless it is thus sterilized.

TREATMENT OF THE CREAM.

Sweet-cream butter has so far not come into demand in Denmark either for home consumption or for export, and there is but little, if any, of that article made. The treatment of the subject is therefore confined to the methods practiced for the production of butter from sour cream. There are two reasons for souring the cream aside from the one that sweet-cream butter finds no sale: First, it is found that sour cream yields more butter than sweet cream, and, second, souring or fermenting the cream is, in accordance with the present standard, thought to increase the aroma and good taste of the butter. Experiments have proved that the difference in yield of butter by the two systems is about 4 per cent, or very nearly equal to the difference of one pound of milk for each pound of butter.

STERILIZATION OF THE CREAM.

The first essential condition to success in butter-making is to have a good quality of cream. It must not be affected by bad odors, nor by bitter, salt, or other offensive taste. These faults may be due to the cows, in which case their milk should be withdrawn from the creamery. Investigations have proved, however, that in the vast majority of instances faulty cream is due to bacteria, many forms of which, both useful and injurious, have been discovered. To counteract their influence it has been the practice in many Danish dairies, during the last three or four years, either to sterilize the cream immediately after it is separated or the milk before separation takes place. How this could be done was first pointed out by the great Frenchman, Pasteur. He showed that by heating the liquid containing these bacteria up to 75° or 80° C., the greater part of them would be killed, and after him the method is frequently called pasteurization. Prof. Fjord was the inventor of the sterilization apparatus, which has already been described and which is in common use; but it is not absolutely necessary to use this machine. The same result can be reached by the use of boiling water, whether this water is heated by steam or in a kettle over the fire. The latter method I saw used in several places with success. In that case the cream is put into tall cylindrical milk cans, which have first been thoroughly cleaned by washing in mild lye, or by the addition of soda to the wash water, or with water containing lime in solution, and thereafter cleaned by a jet of steam, or, if steam cannot be had, scalding water.

The cream cans are sunk to the rim in the hot water, and this is kept near the boiling point either by the constant addition of boiling water or, what is more convenient, by heating it with a jet of steam through a pipe. The cream in the cans is constantly stirred, so that it may warm equally through the mass, care being taken that the paddle used to stir with has been thoroughly cleaned. It is, in most cases, made of galvanized iron. The dairymaid holds in one hand her thermometer immersed in the cream, while with the other she keeps up the stirring, watching the rise of the temperature all the while, and when it reaches 80° C. (176° F.), which temperature should not be exceeded, she lifts the can out and at once immerses it in ice water, where, by continual stirring again, it is cooled as rapidly as possible till it reaches about 35° or 36° F. It can then remain standing in the ice until such time as it is found convenient to begin the fermentation. The sterilizing apparatus differs from this as to result only in that it does the work more rapidly, with greater certainty, and with less labor on behalf of the dairy people. As already described, the cream runs into the bottom of the apparatus from a reservoir, which may be filled directly from the separator, and after being heated by the steam while it is stirred by the agitator in the machine it runs out again at the top in a continuous stream, and the cream is then either cooled by immediately running over one of the coolers described or it may be placed in cans and these be set in ice water. The object of it all is to free the cream from bacteria of all kinds, and then, by the addition of a previously prepared ferment which is known to be pure, to ferment the cream to such a degree that it shall be capable of producing the best quality of butter.

METHODS OF FERMENTATION.

(1) *Natural souring.*—Treating of these in the progressive order in which they have been brought into use, I shall first mention the souring of the cream without attempting to influence the result by artificial means. This is the old-fashioned way. It is still used now and then on small farms, the owners of which have not kept pace with the times. Sterilizing is unknown to this method. When skimmed from the milk cream is at once poured into the cream barrel, which is kept in some corner of the milk room, or, in the colder seasons of the year, may be alongside the stove in the kitchen, or in any warm room where it will be liable to sour quickly. This method, as stated, is now used only in small places; but I mention it here because with careful manipulation the results may be entirely satisfactory, provided that the milk room is clean and sweet, that the milk is from sound cows, that the stable is kept clean and airy, and that there are no contaminating influences outside, such as from stagnant water or manure heaps and the like, which can gain access to the dairy room through the air. This might be styled self-souring, or natural souring. I would not have it understood that all Danish dairies sterilize their cream or milk, for this is far from being the case; they do so only when they find it necessary in order to produce butter of first quality. I visited several places where the conditions were so favorable, the premises kept so clean, that it was not necessary to sterilize the cream at all, but they, nevertheless, fermented the cream by one of the following methods.

(2) *By the use of buttermilk.*—In this case a portion of the buttermilk is taken from the churn immediately after the butter is removed and added to the cream barrel. The quantity used will differ much according to the quantity of cream, the sourness of the buttermilk, and the season of the year, and also with the length of time that the butter-maker desires to give to the fermentation. It is a matter which each butter-maker decides upon for himself according to his experience. But I can say that it does not usually exceed 10 per cent of the cream nor less than 5 per cent. The objections to the use of buttermilk are, that if there is any defect in the churning from which it is taken it will, of course, transmit the same defect to the cream, and the undesirable qualities are thus perpetuated. It is also somewhat more difficult to keep the fermentation under complete control, in that the buttermilk is liable to vary more in acidity than any other form of ferment. If it is found by experience that the buttermilk does not produce the right flavor in the butter, from whatever cause, it is a common practice to resort to a neighboring dairy for the buttermilk; and experience has proved that sometimes this expedient will entirely overcome the injurious influences which affect the cream and butter, and that when this is done once or twice the buttermilk from the home dairy can again be used for some time with entire satisfaction. Before the ferment, of whatever kind, is added the cream should be raised to a temperature

which varies between 70° and 95° F. This is done either by running it through a forewarmer—the apparatus described as being used to heat the milk before it runs into the separator (see Fig. 9)—or by simply immersing the cans of cream in warm water and gently stirring until it reaches the desired temperature. Still another method of warming it is to insert a cylindrical can of small diameter filled with boiling water into the cream can or cream barrel and allowing this to stand until the cream reaches the desired temperature, it being gently stirred in the meantime. In any case the cream should be warmed to the degree mentioned before the buttermilk or other ferment is added. In the cool season of the year precautions are taken to prevent the falling of the temperature too low in the cream barrel until the fermentation is complete. These precautions consist either in keeping the room warm by a stove or steam pipe or in having the cream barrel stand in a box or large barrel prepared for the purpose, so that it can be packed all around with hay, and a similar covering, either a quilt or hay mattress, is put over the lid of the cream barrel. The proper degree of fermentation is usually reached in the course of eighteen to twenty hours. The butter-maker starts the fermentation at such a time that the cream will be ready to churn at the most convenient hour the following day. I found, in most cases, that the fermentation was started at about noon; the cream would then be ready to churn by 6 o'clock the next morning. During this interval it was gently stirred two or three times and the progress of the fermentation watched by the changes in appearance, in taste, and in smell.

(3) *By the use of sour cream.*—Sour cream is occasionally used as a starter. A portion of the cream churned to-day is thus set aside in the morning, and at noon added to the cream that is to be churned to-morrow. Practical butter-makers admit, however, that sour cream is even less desirable than buttermilk, for the reason that, owing to the presence of the fat and off taste which it might have, it is not so readily detected as in the use of buttermilk, and it, in like manner, perpetuates whatever faults there may be from one churning to the next. In all other respects the preparation of the cream for churning is the same as already described.

(4) *By the use of skim milk.*—In the use of both buttermilk and sour cream as a ferment there is a continual perpetuation of the same fermenting elements from week to week, and month to month, as long as continued. It is found that, in many cases, injurious bacteria creep in, and, after a time, the ferment degenerates and fails to produce the good quality of butter that it did at first. This is, in a measure, obviated by the production of fresh ferment every week or two, as the case may require. Such ferment is usually made from half-skimmed milk, that is, milk which has stood from ten to twelve hours and then been skimmed. It is this milk which, by being heated to about 100° F., and then allowed to stand at a temperature of about 70° F. for from

twenty-four to forty hours, according to the season, will develop the ferment, which can be used for souring the cream The milk used for this purpose should be from a nearly fresh cow. Milk from cows about to go dry does not answer the purpose. Good judgment is required on the part of the butter-maker to obtain the right degree of acidity in this ferment. He examines it frequently, smells it, tastes it, and notices its consistency. It should have a certain degree of thickness, and show the formation of small granules, and should have a clear, sharp taste. If it has a bad smell or taste, or if it does not thicken properly, it should be rejected. As soon as it reaches the proper degree of consistency and sourness the fermentation is stopped, by immersing the can containing it into cold water, where it can remain for a few hours, if necessary, before it is added to the cream. The cream is prepared to receive this ferment by being warmed to a degree varying with the season, from 75° to 84° F., or even more. The top of the ferment in the can should then be skimmed off and discarded, as it may be contaminated with bacteria from the air, and from 3 to 5 per cent of the volume of the cream is added to the cream barrel from the remainder. The cream barrel is now covered and kept at a temperature of about 75° F. until it is ready to churn on the following day. The length of time that it stands varies with the season and the temperature in the cream room, from eighteen to twenty-four hours. This, however, is not the invariable method followed.

Sometimes cream is added to the skim milk before the fermentation begins; at other times the milk is not skimmed at all. The result, however, is the same. A new ferment is obtained, which, if the proper care has been exercised in its production, is capable of souring the cream in such a manner that it will produce a first quality of butter. However, this expedient does not always work satisfactorily. If the dairy building or the surroundings are impregnated with injurious bacteria these are sure to infest this new ferment also, and it fails in a short time.

(5) *By the use of pure cultures.*—When all things else fail to produce the desired quality of butter, resort is had to the use of an artificial ferment, the so-called "pure cultures."

The Danish dairy experts have been at work for several years on the isolation and culture of those bacteria which have been found to be the active agents in the fermentation of the cream and, some two or three years ago, success was so far attained that these artificial cultures were offered on the market for use in the creameries; and at the time of my visit last winter there were three laboratories in which these ferments were cultivated and sold. The methods followed in the production of these cultures are secrets belonging to the respective establishments, which will not be divulged. However, it would appear that any good bacteriologist who had studied the question carefully could reach the same result. The bacteria used were obtained from the finest qualities of butter. They have been isolated and experiments have revealed the nutrients needed for their growth and the temperatures at which they can most readily be propagated. I do not think that any of them claim to know all there is to be known on the subject. They steadily discover that improvements can be made by slight alterations in the methods and that new bacteria heretofore unknown are added to the list. It is certain that the different species of bacteria produce notably different results in the taste and aroma of the cream and butter. Mr. E. A. Quist, of Skanderborg, uses only two species, very distinct in appearance and in the quality they impart to the butter. They are cultivated separately and mixed just before they are sent out to the customers. Blauenfeldt & Tvede, on the other hand, use several kinds in their ferment, which may or may not include those used by Mr. Quist. The results of the use of these pure cultures have been so eminently satisfactory in practice that I found them in very common use. A new starter of these cultures is not needed every day or even every week; and as they are sold reasonably cheap, the expense connected with their use is but slight. When used according to directions sent with them they insure the production of a first quality of butter, which is of greater consideration than the expense their purchase involves. The three laboratories I have mentioned prescribe different methods of procedure in their use, which proves that there is no hard and fast rule that must be followed in order to obtain the desired results. That is, there is a possibility of the extension of this science far beyond our present knowledge of the subject. These artificial cultures are used more particularly in dairies which seem to be infected with injurious bacteria and, to attain the best results, the cream should be sterilized before the ferment is added. The pure culture is added to a small portion of sterilized milk or cream, and then set aside at a given temperature until it has attained the proper growth. It is then further propagated in a still larger quantity of milk or cream and, when a sufficient quantity has been obtained, it is added to the cream in the cream barrel, where it accomplishes the desired fermentation in from eighteen to twenty hours. At the time of my visit none of the laboratories had succeeded in devising means to perpetuate the ferment outside the laboratory for any length of time. It was, therefore, a difficult matter to obtain pure cultures for transmission to America. The preparation required for their transportation during two or three days would not answer the purpose when the journey was extended to as many weeks. I am convinced, however, that it will not be long before this difficulty will be overcome.

There are a few points in the treatment of the cream concerning which no definite directions can be given. One of these is the per cent of ferment, whatever kind is used, which should be added to produce the best results. This depends upon so many things that no definite rule can be given. It depends upon the sourness of the ferment when it is added, upon the length of time it is desired to have the cream stand before it is churned, and upon the temperature which it is practicable to maintain; and in the adjustment of these to one another the butter-maker must follow his own judgment and experience. It is a well-known fact that the fermentation proceeds more rapidly in warm weather than in cold weather, and in summer the process, therefore, usually takes a shorter time than it does in winter. It is essential that the cream should stand in a room with fresh air. In damp and musty air the cream will be sure to lack the aroma and pleasant taste which are so highly prized. It is a maxim in Danish dairying that to obtain the finest quality of butter, which shall keep well, the fermentation must be strong, and that it should not be stopped until the cream has become thick and shows a peculiar granular appearance and at the same time develops the pleasant aroma belonging to good butter. When this point is reached the cream should be churned.

CHURNING.

I saw but one pattern of the churn, and this has already been described. Years ago, before the dairy had reached its present perfection of methods, the old-fashioned dash churn was common in the small dairies. It then required the united aid of the entire household to keep it going at the requisite speed until butter "came." On the large farms the churn with the revolving dasher has always been the favorite, and is the one still in use. The churn is scalded inside with boiling water and immediately afterwards rinsed in fresh cold water before the cream is poured in. The cream should be of the temperature which experience has proved to be the best for the season of the year. This temperature may vary from 50° to 70° F. Thus, milk from cows that are about to go dry requires to be churned at a higher temperature than that from fresh cows. The usual temperature at which to churn is between 55° and 60° F. The quantity of cream should be known in order that the right quantity of butter color can be added. This quantity differs with the demands of the markets, the quality of the color used, and the feed given the cows; so that no rule whatever can be laid down, and there is no uniformity in the Danish practice in this particular. The English market, where practically all the surplus butter is sent, demands that it shall be of a rather light straw color, and so well do the producers meet this demand, under the varying conditions, that it is only the expert eye that can detect differences in the color of the butter from different parts of the country when collected in the warehouses of the wholesale dealers. I saw this practically illustrated in London.

When all conditions are right the length of time taken in churning varies from thirty to forty minutes, but the time, too, is dependent upon several conditions. It depends upon the speed at which the dasher is revolved, upon the construction of the dasher, and upon the condition of the cream, both as to consistency and temperature. The kind of feed given the cattle also has an influence upon it. The higher the temperature, the shorter the time required; but all butter-makers with whom I came in contact were agreed that it is better to churn at a too low than at a too high temperature, as the grain of the butter will, in the latter case, be spoiled. There is, however, danger of getting the temperature too low, especially towards fall when the cows begin to go dry and the weather gets cooler. It is then often the case that the cream will froth and the butter refuse to "come." This is obviated by raising the temperature above the normal. In obstinate cases of this kind it is a common practice to stop the churn and let the cream stand until the following day when it is warmed some 5° or 6° higher than usual and again churned, when the difficulty is generally overcome. The temperature of the cream is watched from time to time as the churning proceeds, and for this purpose there is a hole in the lid through which a thermometer can be dipped into the churn. Usually the agitation of the cream causes the temperature to rise some 3° to 5° in the course of thirty minutes. This is as it ought to be, but if the rise is much greater than that it is an indication that the cream was not at the proper temperature when the churn was started. The formation of the first granules of butter is carefully watched for, and for this purpose there is a short piece of wood or stick with a deep furrow on one side put through a hole in the lid, in which it fits closely. This is removed from time to time to see the size of the granules as they collect in the groove. It is of the utmost importance that the churn be stopped at the right time. If continued longer than necessary the grain of the butter is injured. It is the usual practice, when the granules are about as large as small peas, to stop the churn and to add a small quantity of cold water which is thrown upon the lid and down the sides of the churn, after which the dasher is again started at a slow motion until the butter is sufficiently gathered.

TREATMENT OF THE BUTTER.

The first thing the butter-maker does after the churn is stopped is to wash down the sides of the churn with fresh cold water. In some places boiled water which has again been reduced to normal temperature is used for this purpose. This is to avoid contaminating the butter with bacteria which the water may contain. Perfectly pure well or spring water is, however, used without first being boiled. The churn is invariably stopped while the butter is still in small granules or pellets. The butter is next removed from the churn, which is done as follows: The churn is tipped, as shown in Fig. 15, and with a sieve the butter is gathered as it floats in the buttermilk and transferred to a tub by the side, allowing the buttermilk to drain through the sieve as much as it will. Usually a fine hair sieve is used. Finally the buttermilk is run through a strainer in order to collect the last floating particles of butter. In some places I noticed that it was the practice to dip each sieve full of butter into a tub of clean, cool water, and let this drain through the sieve, thereby washing out a portion of the buttermilk. This, however, is not a common practice. Formerly the butter was sometimes washed in the churn before it was removed, the buttermilk first having been drained off, but this, too, is now obsolete. The Danes believe that butter so washed absorbs too much water, and is less liable to keep.

The next operation consists in pressing the buttermilk out of the butter. In former times this was always done in the butter trough shown in Fig. 16, and by the hands only, or simply by the use of a large wooden paddle made for the purpose. Now, in comparatively few dairies is the butter touched with the hands, and in that case a lump weighing perhaps 8 or 10 pounds is taken up with both hands and put against the sides of the trough, pressed gently with the palms of the hands five or six times, the ends of the flattened mass being turned in after each pressure. In most places the butter-worker is used and is permitted to run under the valve three or four times. When the hands are used, the greatest care is taken that they are clean and cool. They are washed frequently and thoroughly and they are always dipped in cold water before the butter is touched. This is essential, not only to cool the hands, but to prevent the butter from sticking to the fingers, and the same precaution is taken with all the utensils with which the butter comes in contact. Everything is scrubbed first in boiling water to sterilize the implements, and next in clean cool water.

As soon as the buttermilk has been removed the butter is weighed in order to calculate the amount of salt required, and the salt is worked in at this time, always on the butter-worker. Sometimes it is put in at one working, and in other places it is preferred to add it in two workings. The amount of salt used I found was not uniform. It was adapted to the taste of the market where it was expected to be sold, but it varies between 4 and 5 per cent of the weight of the butter. The salt is not weighed, but measured in a large glass with a scale graduated to grams on the side, 5 grams being equal to 1 per cent. Usually the butter is sold, as I shall explain later, to butter dealers, who handle it either on commission or they buy it outright on their own account. These dealers are supposed to know the wants of the market, and it is customary to accept their instructions in regard to the amount of salt and color to be added to the butter. The salt is worked into the butter with the least possible amount of handling, and it is then laid aside for some time before the next working takes place. In summer it is put in the butter-coolers already described (see Fig. 17), which are a sort of ice box. In winter it may simply be laid in large rolls in the butter trough or on a table provided for the purpose. It lies here for at least two hours in the cold season, and when the weather is warm it may lie for eight or ten hours, or even until in the cool of the following morning, before it receives the final working. The object is, not only to cool the butter, and thus allow it to become firmer, but also to allow the salt to dissolve and to penetrate the whole mass. When it has attained the proper degree of firmness it is again put under the butter-worker, and the last buttermilk and a considerable portion of the brine formed from the salt is worked out. How much working it can stand differs much in individual cases. Care is taken, however, that it is not the least bit overworked so as to become greasy and sticky. This working may be repeated a couple of times, or it may be packed for shipment at once; practice is not uniform on this point. It is common, however, to give it one more working an hour or two later. The main point is not to work it until it has become decidedly firm, and then work it only to the extent it can bear without injuring the grain, and yet remove as much as possible of the brine which has formed from the dissolving salt. It is worthy of notice that although 4 per cent of salt may be added, with proper working about half of this is removed in the form of brine.

PACKING FOR MARKET.

The Danish butter is invariably packed in barrels. These may vary in size according to the demands of the market, but they are always of the same pattern. One of these barrels and the wooden mallet used to pack the butter firmly in it are represented in the accompanying illustration (Fig. 19). The most usual size is one which will contain an English hundredweight (112 pounds), but this size is not uniform. These barrels are usually manufactured on the farm where they are to be used, the "feed-master" combining with this important office the trade of a cooper. While the cows are eating he makes the butter barrels. These barrels are usually made of beech wood. The European beech wood is white, fine grained and hard,

FIG. 19.—Barrel in which butter is packed for market.

and of course it is thoroughly seasoned. The staves are held together by wooden hoops and the barrel is made perfectly smooth inside. The day before it is to be filled with butter it is first thoroughly scrubbed in scalding water and next filled with clean cold water, which remains standing in it until a short time before it is wanted. It is next rubbed with salt all over the inside, letting as much as possible adhere to the sides. The bottom and sides are next lined with paraffin paper to prevent the butter coming into contact with the wood. Then the butter is packed in lumps of 10 and 12 pounds, and by the use of the mallet it is pressed firmly down in order to prevent any openings in it. This process is continued until the barrel is full. It is filled slightly higher than will permit the putting on of the lid, and with a sharp, flat spoon the excess is cut off to just the point required to admit the lid. Now a sheet of paraffin paper is put over it and this is covered with a thin layer of fine salt. The lid is then put on, the hoops tightened, and the barrel is ready for market. During the time it remains in the creamery it is placed in a cool storeroom, usually adjacent to the ice house, until enough has been collected for shipment to the dealer. It is customary in most dairies to ship their export butter to the agent about once a week.

USE OF SKIM MILK AND BUTTERMILK.

Much of the skim milk is used for cheese. Considerable is also used in the household, and what is not used for these purposes is fed to calves and pigs. It is customary in feeding calves to gradually substitute skim milk for whole milk, after the first two weeks. As the older cows drop out of the herd, or cease to be profitable, their places are taken by young stock raised on the place. It is customary, also, to keep a number of swine, which are fed, for the most part, on the offal from the dairy. In the coöperative dairies the farmers who furnish the milk take back the skim milk, this being, in most cases, a part of the contract, and in some cases the buttermilk is in like manner returned to the producer at a moderate valuation. These products are then used in the same manner as on the larger farms. Near the towns there is always a good market for skim milk among the poor people, who can buy it at a low rate. It will thus be seen that nothing is wasted, everything is utilized, and it is to be noted that the skim milk is returned to the producer while it is sweet. In no case did I find the stinking skim-milk reservoir which seems to be a fixture in American creameries, and from which our farmers help themselves. The skim milk is also fed to colts with good results.

DESCRIPTION OF PLACES VISITED.

In what follows I shall attempt to give some idea of the methods followed on Danish dairy farms, both in the dairy and in the production of crops. Of course many details have been overlooked, but it is hoped that enough has been gathered to give the reader a fairly correct notion of the system manifest in the work, and the care given to details. I was compelled, for lack of time, to confine myself to the salient points in farming methods. Had more time been at my disposal it would have been possible to have gone more into details, but I could usually spend only one day at a place, and this, too, at a season when there was practically no farm work going on.

THE MILK-SUPPLY COMPANY OF COPENHAGEN.

I took early occasion to visit the city milk-supply station of Copenhagen, which I shall briefly describe. I am aware that it has already been partially described in our agricultural press, but it is an institution of such extraordinary interest, owing to the methods there adopted in handling milk, that it will bear further mention, and should serve as the worthy example for our many large cities to follow. It is in the hands and under the exclusive control of a private organization. Neither the Government nor city has anything whatever to do with it. It should also be explained that it does not by any means supply all the milk consumed in Copenhagen. Just what part it supplies of the total amount consumed in the city I am unable to state, but it is considerably less than one-fourth. The Milk-supply Company of Copenhagen is simply an organization which has taken upon itself to supply its patrons with absolutely pure and wholesome milk at a slightly advanced price above what milk can be bought for from the numerous other sources of supply. The company began business some fifteen years ago on a small scale, but for the month of December, 1879, the daily sales averaged 9,733 Danish pounds (10,728 pounds avoirdupois), and for December, 1892, 36,194 Danish pounds (39,896 pounds avoirdupois), and this at the season when milk is scarcest. The merit of the system consists, first, in the strict rules which have been laid down concerning the quality of the milk; second, in the painstaking cleanliness which obtains in the handling of the milk; and, third, in the unflinching enforcement of the rules mentioned. Each dairy farmer of whom the company buys the milk must agree to conform to the following requirements in every particular:

(1) The feed must be such that it does not affect the taste or character of the milk injuriously. The use of distillery slop and like substances for feed is absolutely prohibited, and the use of all feed that has been injured or is not well preserved. The use of turnips, kohlrabi, rutabagas, and the leaves of all kinds of root crops is prohibited. Carrots and mangels may be used to the extent of half a bushel per day for each cow, but only when the grain feed given amounts to 7 pounds per day. Cows which supply milk for the use of children must not be fed mangels and carrots beyond the extent of 1 peck per day. Oil cake (rape-seed cakes) may be fed to the extent of but 1½ pounds per day, and this only in connection with at least 5 pounds of grain feed. Cows supplying milk for the use of children must not be fed oil cake of any kind. For other cows the grain mixture used shall receive the company's approval before delivery of milk can begin.

(2) In the summer time the cows must not be fed in the barn under any conditions. They must be pastured on clover and grass. Vetches must not be used. When necessary, arrangements may be made with the company for the use of grain or green grain crops during the summer.

(3) The cows must be clipped on the udder, tail, and hind quarters in the fall before they are put in the barn.

(4) The time of calving of cows in the herd must be distributed as evenly as possible through the year, so that the amount of milk delivered, especially during September and October, shall not be less than two-thirds of the greatest amount delivered in any month.

(5) Fresh milk up to twelve days after calving must not be delivered, nor will the company receive milk from cows which give less than 6 pounds per day.

(6) The utmost cleanliness must be observed in milking, and the milk must be strained through a metal strainer covered with a clean woolen cloth.

(7) There must be at the disposal of the dairy at least 30 pounds of ice for every 100 pounds of milk produced on the farm.

(8) Every dairy must be supplied with a Lawrence milk-cooler. This may be rented from the company if desired.

(9) As soon as it is drawn from the cow, the milk must be cooled by the use of ice water on the milk cooler, and this at all seasons of the year. This cooling should reduce the temperature of the milk to at least 4° Réaumur (41° F.) before it is shipped.

(10) The milk must be delivered at the railway station once or twice daily, as the company may desire, either as sweet milk or as half-skimmed milk and cream. It must not be sent from the dairy farm sooner than necessary to make the train, and in summer the delivery wagon must be covered so as to shade the cans.

(11) The company will supply the cans used for transportation, and they will be cleaned before they are shipped to the dairy farm.

(12) The cans must be rinsed in cold water immediately on their arrival at the dairy. They must be kept in an airy place, protected from all dirt, with the lids removed and opening downward, but so that the air has free access to the interior, until they are used.

(13) The can must under no circumstances be used for anything else than the transportation of milk.

(14) The dairy farmer must agree to answer all questions which the company may put to him concerning the milk.

(15) The dairy farmer must permit one of the company's veterinarians to examine his cattle whenever he chooses, and must carry out the directions which the latter may give him. He must also agree to furnish transportation for the veterinarian to and from the railroad station.

(16) Cows which the veterinarian finds have tuberculosis must be removed from the herd at once and disposed of as soon as possible.

(17) Cows which are taken with any suspicious disease must be removed from the herd at once and the company informed of the fact, and, if necessary, the delivery of milk may be stopped until the veterinarian has had opportunity to examine the case. But in such cases the company will pay for the milk at the same rate as though it were delivered.

(18) If any contagious disease occurs among the persons who live on the farm, or at the homes of the laborers who work on the farm, it shall be the duty of the dairyman to inform the company of the fact at once. The milk will, in such cases, be paid for at the usual rate.

(19) This contract may be terminated either by the company or the dairyman on the first day of any year, but with at least six months' notice.

(20) Should the milk be found to be of such an inferior quality as to be unfit for sale, the company reserves the right to stop its delivery without remuneration.

(21) If the sale of milk in Copenhagen should be stopped by reason of an epidemic or other non-preventable cause, the delivery must be stopped for a shorter or longer period without remuneration.

This very strict code is observed to the letter. At present the company receives milk from 42 dairy farms, representing in round numbers 4,600 milch cows. To watch the health of these cows the company employs three skilled veterinarians, who spend all their time in traveling from farm to farm in order to examine periodically each individual in the herds, and also to see that the rules as regards feeding, etc., are observed. When an animal is found to be suffering from any sort of disease, it is withdrawn at once. And should a disease occur suddenly the dairyman is encouraged in withdrawing of his own accord the animals so affected, and is paid the price of the milk which they give until one of the company's veterinarians can pass judgment on the case.

In addition to this the company employs a staff of trained dairymaids who travel from farm to farm, call unexpectedly, examine the surrounding conditions with special reference to cleanliness and care in milking, watch the feeding, the cooling of the milk, etc., and then promptly report the facts they obtain to the company on blanks furnished them for the purpose. On some of the larger farms such dairymaids are permanently located, the company paying the dairymen for their board. At present there are four such dairywomen located on as many farms. But the inspection does not end here. At the receiving station in Copenhagen a sample of the milk from each farm is taken immediately on its arrival and subjected to the Babcock test, a large machine of this pattern having been procured for that purpose a short time ago, and once or twice a month similar samples are subjected to chemical analysis. Moreover, when the sample is taken an experienced dairywoman stands by, who tastes and smells of the milk from each farm, and who quickly notes whether it falls below the high standard that is required.

I spent a night and the greater part of two days at the company's receiving and distributing station in order to watch its operations. Including the drivers of delivery wagons and the boys who assist them by carrying the milk from the wagon to the house, the number of employees is about 250. The milk is shipped to the city in the evening. The trains begin to arrive about 9 p. m., and continue until after midnight. The milk is at once hauled to this receiving station or dairy, where it is weighed, sampled, tasted, and the cans deposited in large vats of ice water, where they remain till 4 a. m., when the delivery wagons begin to make ready.

The cans are of tin, made very massive, and hold about 100 pounds each. Two forms are used, one round,.the other square. The round cans are used for the unskimmed milk and the square cans for the half-skimmed milk. Otherwise they are shaped like a jug, with contracted neck, into which a lid fits very closely. In the interior of the cans for unskimmed milk is an arrangement intended to equalize the distribution of the cream with the milk. It will be seen that when a can of sweet milk stands on a delivery wagon several hours the upper stratum of milk must be richer in cream than the lower stratum, and that if the milk is drawn from the bottom the first customer will practically get skim-milk and the last cream. To prevent such injustice, the tube, or pipe, in which the discharge valve is placed is continued clear to the top of the can on the inside, and a row of small holes the whole length of this tube admits the milk. Now, when the valve is opened, the milk is drawn neither from the bottom nor top of the can, exclusively, but through these small holes in the tube—from the whole side of the can from bottom to top, or as high as the milk may reach, equally. The weight of each can is stamped upon a brass plate which is soldered to the top of the can. This greatly facilitates weighing. Before leaving the farm each can is sealed with a cord and a piece of lead stamped with a punch, in the same manner as our railroad freight cars are sealed. This precludes all possibility of tampering with the contents in transit, and a label bearing the name of the farm in large print is also pasted on each can.

The company supplies its customers with three grades of milk, namely, whole milk, half skim milk, and milk for children, and with two grades of cream, designated respectively as first and second grade. The skim milk received, and for which there is a large demand for use in cooking, is in most cases the morning's milk which has stood ten to twelve hours before shipment. The cream that may have risen is then skimmed off and shipped in separate cans. The children's milk is intended as food for infants. For this supply special cows are picked by the company's veterinarians, and these are fed somewhat differently, or at least with greater care than the others, and their milk is kept separate. This milk is filtered and bottled and the bottles sealed immediately on arrival, and not allowed to stand in the cans till morning, as is the other milk. The ordinary whole and skim milk is also filtered before it goes to the customer, but this is done at 4 a. m., just before it is loaded into the delivery wagons.

The filtering machines are of special interest. There are several of them, and they vary somewhat in size, but otherwise the construction is the same. Imagine a large bowl of enameled iron with a capacity of about 40 gallons, and this raised on supports about 5 feet from the floor. There is a hole in the bottom through which the milk enters, and near the rim are two discharge pipes, one on each side of the bowl. Now, the filtering material consists of three layers of gravel and six thicknesses of fine muslin stretched over a ring that fits closely inside the bowl and is placed above the upper layer of gravel. The gravel is of three grades of fineness. The lower is about the size of buckshot, the middle layer finer still, and the upper layer as fine as small pinheads. Each layer rests upon a tin plate, perforated with many fine holes, and which fits closely to the sides of the bowl. Each layer is about 2 inches thick, and there is a space of an inch from the top of one layer to the tin plate which supports the next layer above. The milk is poured into a large reservoir which stands somewhat higher than the filter. A brass pipe leads from the bottom of this reservoir to the bottom of the filter bowl. The pressure thus attained forces the milk through the succesive layers of gravel and the six thicknesses of cloth, and when it rises to the discharge pipes it runs off through these into the vessels placed for its reception. Such treatment throughout assures the customer that it is absolutely pure, clean, and wholesome.

Probably no other city in the world is blessed with so thorough a system of control as regards the quality of the milk. And be it noted that it is not done under compulsion of law, but as a piece of business enterprise in private hands. The constitution of the company forbids a greater dividend than 5 per cent, and the price to the consumer is regulated on this basis. It further prohibits the two principal directors from having any financial interest in the company which might tempt them to work for greater profits. The prices paid to the producer for the milk are as follows: From the 1st of April to the 1st of September 20 öre* per "Kande" (2 kilograms=4,409 pounds avoirdupois), which is very nearly $1.25 per hundred pounds avoirdupois. From September 1 to December 16, 26 öre per 2 kilograms, or $1.61 per 100 pounds, and from December 16 to April 1, 22 öre per 2 kilograms, or $1.36 per 100 pounds. This is for the ordinary sweet milk. Milk for children costs rather more and skim milk correspondingly less. The company retails this milk from its wagons in the street at the following rates: Milk for children at 10 öre per half kilogram, ordinary milk at 8 öre per half kilogram, and skim milk and buttermilk at 4 öre per half kilogram, which is approximately 5½ cents per quart for children's milk, 4½ cents per quart for sweet milk, and 2¼ cents per quart for skim-milk and buttermilk. The cream is sold at 27 cents per quart for first quality and 16½ cents per quart for second quality. The cream which is not sold is made into butter, and in like manner the whole milk which is returned from the wagons is creamed and the skim milk resulting sold to poor people at half price.

Pay of employees—Their method of treating their employees is interesting, to say the least, and I think it contains a lesson not unworthy the attention of employers of this country. The company has in its employ, altogether, some 250 persons. Most of these are drivers of milk wagons and drivers' assistants, boys who carry the milk from the wagon to the house; but there are also a number of skilled dairy people, clerks, etc. The pay of all is graded to the character of the work; but it is the policy of the company to retain faithful servants as long as possible, and this they do by liberal treatment. The pay of a clerk, for instance, is about $43 a month; but on New Year's day he gets a present of about $54 besides; and each clerk who can show an increase in his bank account of not less than about $2.70 per month gets about $1.35 more deposited to his credit in the bank. In the same manner each driver or other working man who can show a monthly increase of about 54 cents in his bank account gets about 54 cents more deposited to his credit in the bank. This money remains at compound inter-

---

*The unit of Danish money is the crown (krone), which contains 100 öre. One dollar is at present worth 3 crowns and 65 öre, and one cent is consequently equal to 3.65 öre.

est for a certain number of years, and by the time it becomes available it amounts to a substantial sum, which may help the owner to a home or enable him to open a business. The regular wages of a driver is from about 70 to 80 cents a day, but in addition to this he gets a commission on the milk sold of one-half öre for each Danish pound, the commission being the same for both sweet and skim milk, and at the end of the year he gets a commission of 1 öre for each pound of butter he has taken orders for during the year. By these means the company not only gets efficient servants but it retains them, and through its encouragements to work and to save it has a beneficial influence on all its employees. The credit for this model plan of supplying a large city with milk belongs to Grosserer Busk, of Copenhagen, more than to any other one man. He has been the leading spirit of the company from its inception and organization to the present day.

LARGE DAIRY FARMS.

ROSENFELDT FARM.

The first large dairy farm I had opportunity to visit is named Rosenfeldt, which is situated near the city of Vordinborg. It is the property of a Danish nobleman, Kammerherre Oxholm, who lives on the place. The farm contains 1,300 acres. The actual number of cows on the place was 276, which number was, however, to be increased to upwards of 300 by the addition of heifers which were soon to come in. Of the above number of cows 223 were in milk at the time of my visit, and they produced, on an average, 3,747 pounds of milk per day. This gives but an average of 17 pounds per day per cow, or about 2 gallons. If this seems a small output it should be remembered that it was in midwinter, when many of them were about to go dry, and that the native Danish dairy cow is but a small animal. The average weight would not much exceed 900 pounds per head. When these things are taken into consideration the milk yield was not small. These cattle were fed as follows: The first feed was given them at 4 o'clock in the morning and consisted of oat straw or barley straw. They got a liberal amount, and what was left was used for bedding. At 7 a. m. they were fed their grain, which averaged about 7 pounds per head per day, divided into two feeds, and consisted of 3 pounds barley and oats mixed and crushed, 2 pounds oil cake, usually half rapeseed cake and half palm cake or sunflower cake (of rapeseed cake they never fed more than $1\frac{1}{2}$ pounds), and 2 pounds bran. At 8:30 a. m. they got 20 pounds sugar-beet refuse each. The beets are grown on the farm and delivered to a neighboring sugar factory, but the refuse pulp is hauled back for feed. Or if the pulp is missing mangels are fed instead. Next they are watered in the stable, the water being turned right into the mangers, and after this they get 10 pounds each of hay from the meadow. The hay is of mixed grasses, containing also some clover. This completes the feeding for the forenoon. At 1 p. m. the feeding begins again with the same feeds in the same quantities, beginning first with the grain, then roots, water, hay, and straw, keeping them busy eating all the afternoon, the straw being fed at 7 p. m., and this time wheat straw.

The milking begins at 4 o'clock in the morning and at 4 o'clock in the afternoon. It is all done by women, each of whom milks 20 cows, and they do it in from two to two and one-half hours. The churning temperature is 55° F., and butter comes in about thirty minutes.

The particular ferment which was used in this dairy received the following treatment: It is sold in bottles holding about a pint, all of which is used at one time. It it not added directly to the cream, but is first propagated in skim-milk. For this purpose the milk from a fresh cow should, if possible, be selected. The milk is set in ice water for twelve hours and then skimmed by hand. It is next sterilized by being heated to 180° F., at which temperature it should be kept for two hours. It is then cooled to 82° F. and the bottle of ferment is added, and this temperature should, as far as practicable, be maintained during the next twenty or twenty-four hours while the ferment is growing, which takes about that time. At the close of this process another batch of skim milk is sterilized as before. It is next cooled to 50° F., then again warmed to 82° F., and 10 per cent of its weight is added to it from the ferment made the previous day. This stands again another twenty-four hours at the same temperature as nearly as may be, and then it is ready to be added to the cream, for which purpose the cream should be at 70° F.

A herdsman styled "feed master" has charge of the feeding. The milk is, of course, weighed as fast as it arrives at the dairy, but twice a month there is a "trial milking," at which the milk is weighed from each cow, which enables them to get an approximately correct idea of the yield of each cow. The cows do not get out of the barn all winter. When tied up in the fall they remain there till they are put in pasture the following spring, which usually occurs the latter part of May. This, I find, is the practice on nearly all dairy farms.

The morning milk is run through the separator as fast as it arrives in the dairy from the barn, and the evening milk stands in the vat and is separated also in the morning.

The cream runs from the separator into the "pasteurizing" or sterilizing apparatus, where it is heated to 167° F., after which it is at once cooled on the cooling apparatus to 44° F. This heating and cooling is completed by about half past 7 in the morning, and from that hour until 10 a. m. it stands in ice water. It is then heated again, but this time only to 70° F., at which temperature the prepared cream ferment is added, and it now stands for about twenty hours, or until 6 a. m. the next morning, while the ferment does its work, and then it is churned. The amount of ferment added to the cream will in a measure depend upon the season, the cows, and other conditions. In the dairy to which this refers it was found that of this impregnated milk 4 to 5 per cent of the weight of the cream should be added at this season to have the proper effect. The ferment is perpetuated in sterilized skim milk, which is prepared fresh every day, and what is made one day is used the next day both to ferment the cream and to start a new lot in fresh skim milk. On Mr. Oxholm's dairy farm it is found necessary to get a fresh lot of ferment from the laboratory about once in six weeks.

I have briefly described the process followed on this farm because the butter made there stands in high repute. It frequently takes prizes at the national butter exhibits, and I was told that it brought usually about $1.62 per 100 pounds above the top market quotation. It is all exported to England. Nearly all the work in this dairy is done by women, and the chief dairymaid was certainly a competent person. Most of the skim milk was made into cheese of good quality. It is possible to make good cheese from skim milk, but the success lies in the knowing how, and I believe the time is coming when good skim-milk cheese will find a market in America.

At Rosenfeldt it required at this season 29 pounds of milk to make a pound of butter. The cream loses some of its butter by being sterilized as it was here.

About 1,000 pounds of skim milk was made into cheese daily, and the remaining skim milk was sterilized and fed to the calves and pigs. The cheese milk was warmed to 70° F. When it reached this temperature 10 per cent of fresh buttermilk was added—that is, 100 pounds to the 1,000 pounds of milk—and immediately afterwards rennet of a given strength was added. In this case it required seventeen one-hundredths of a pound of rennet for the amount of milk used. After the rennet had been stirred in, the milk was allowed to stand perfectly still until it had coagulated, which happened, usually, in about thirty minutes. The chief dairymaid informed me that if it coagulated in less than twenty minutes the cheese would be tough, and if it took over forty minutes in winter, the milk got too cool. The time when the desired degree of coagulation was reached was determined by inserting the finger and noticing how readily the cheese matter would break when the finger was gently lifted up through it from below. A certain brittleness was a sign that the process had proceeded far enough. The curd was then cut both ways with wire cutters and allowed to stand five minutes undisturbed, but at the end of this time it was stirred gently and continuously from twenty to thirty minutes. This stirring separated the curd from the whey. The whey was then drawn off and the curd was worked with the hands and pressed in the bottom of the cheese vat until all the whey that could be separated by this process was removed.

Four per cent of salt was next added to the curd and thoroughly mixed through it with the hands. The cheese cups were then filled and the cheeses were put under light pressure for twenty hours, being turned three times during that period. On removal from the press they were put into a large tub of strong brine, so strong that the cheese would swim on the surface, and allowed to remain there from twelve to fourteen hours. On removal from the brine they were placed upon shelves in the cheese room, where a temperature is maintained of from 56° to 60° F. They remained there fourteen days, during which time they were daily turned and wiped on both sides with a cloth. After two weeks of this treatment they were transferred to another room where the temperature was kept lower than in the cheese room, and there kept until sold. During the first few weeks in this room they were washed every other day in strong brine, the object being to make the crust soft and thin. They were usually sold when about three months old and brought in the home market 19 öre per Danish pound, which is equal to about 5 cents per pound avoirdupois.

All the dairy work was in the direct charge of the chief dairymaid, who had half a dozen assistants, most of whom were pupils. The farm was managed by a superintendent, a scientifically educated gentleman and a graduate from the Royal Agricultural School of Copenhagen. He had several assistants. As stated, the farm consisted of about 1,300 acres, and it required 18 teams (36 horses) and 8 yoke of oxen to work it. The rotation observed at that time was as follows: First year, fallow, this being manured for the next year's crop; second year, rye or wheat; third, barley; fourth, sugar beets; fifth, barley; sixth, oats; seventh and eighth, clover and grass. But the superintendent informed me that it was contemplated to change the rotation to this: First year, rye or wheat; second year, one-third in potatoes, one-third in beans, and one-third in peas; third year, barley; fourth year, sugar beets; fifth, barley; sixth, oats; seventh and eighth, clover and grass. All of the land is fall-plowed and the manure is applied for the wheat and rye. Occasionally, also, artificial manure for the sugar beets.

On all of these large farms we find young men who are there to learn the business of farming. They may remain one or two years, according to contract, and some of them receive a small wage when they consent to eat at the tables with the hired men and in other respects "hoe their row" alongside the hired men. Others are there without any pay, and still others pay for the privilege of being there.

On this farm there were two classes of farm pupils, one class receiving 100 crowns a year in wages (about $27) and the other class receiving no pay. All were required to work alike, however, and they were expected to work as steadily and hard as was required of the hired men, the only difference in their privileges being that they got their meals in a separate room. The hired men who worked on the farm received 200 crowns a year ($54) and their board, and day laborers received from 36 to 37 cents per day, boarding themselves.

AUNÖ FARM.

This farm also belongs to Kammerherre Oxholm, the owner of Rosenfeldt, already described, but it was tenanted by Mr. Stolpe, who had rented the farm for a series of years. The farm is some 700 acres in extent and was worked on a system of mixed husbandry, with special attention to dairying. At the time of my visit there were 260 cows on the farm, 50 of which were dry. An average of 3,000 pounds of milk per day was obtained from the 210 cows giving milk, and in addition to this 1,000 pounds per day were bought from neighboring farmers. The total amount of milk was, therefore, 4,000 pounds per day. The dairy work was in charge of a man, but the milking, cleaning of utensils, etc., was done by women. The feeding of the cattle was in charge of a so-called feed-master, who is also the cooper and makes the butter barrels. The cows were fed as follows: The first feed was given them at 4 a. m., and consisted of either oat straw or barley straw. The milking was done while this was being eaten. At 7 they were watered, after which they received a small feed of chaff. When this was eaten they got their grain, consisting of 1 pound of bran, 3 pounds of barley and oats ground together, and 1 pound of rape-seed cake. Half an hour later they each got 10 pounds of mangels and next a feed of hay. This completed the feeding for the forenoon. At 1 p. m. they were again watered and then followed in succession feeds of chaff, grain (the same as above), mangels, hay, and straw, the last feed being given about 6 in the evening. Milking was done about twelve hours apart, beginning at 4 in the morning and again at 4 o'clock in the evening. All the cattle remained in the barn during the entire winter, the water also being given them in the mangers. The cattle were of the red Danish dairy breed, with some crosses of the Angler breed. The evening milk was put in tall, tin milk cans, which were set in cold water over night. In the morning these were skimmed by hand and the milk, which had thus stood only twelve hours, was run through a separator, together with the morning's milk. The milk ran through a forewarmer, a machine already described, which raised it to 95° F., before it ran into the separator. The cream, as it came from the separator, ran into large milk cans which were at once immersed in ice water and cooled under constant stirring to about 35° F., and here it remained until it was again warmed for the reception of the ferment and set to sour in the cream barrels. They occasionally used artificial cream ferments and occasionally they made their own ferment from half-skimmed milk. The method followed on this place for the production of the latter was as follows: The evening milk from a nearly fresh cow was set by itself in ice water over night and in the morning was skimmed. The skim milk was warmed to 170° F., and then cooled to between 72° and 75° F., at which temperature it remained for twenty-four hours, when it was found to be sour. Of this sour milk 5 per cent of the weight of the cream was added to the cream which had been separated in the morning and cooled off in ice water, as already stated. The cream was warmed to 70° F., before the sour milk was added, and it was, as far as possible, kept at this temperature until 6 the following morning, being gently stirred two or three times in the meantime.

During the winter the churning temperature was at 62° F., and the cream rose to 66° F. during the process of churning. In the summer, I was informed, they churned at 50° F., or a little above, according to the weather, and butter always came in from thirty to thirty-five minutes.

The crops on the farm consisted chiefly of barley, oats, rye, and a little wheat, and besides these, mangels for the cattle, some potatoes, grasses and clover. Of the grains only so much was sold as could be spared from the amount necessary to keep the live stock. The tenant, Mr. Stolpe, was an able farmer, and in spite of the fact that the rent of the farm came to some $1,890 per year, he managed to pay all the expenses and still put something in the bank, the dairy being the main source of income.

THUREBYLILLE FARM.

This farm can also be classed among the large estates. It contains an area of a little over 700 acres, of which some 60 acres are in permanent meadow, and the rest under culture. The farm was owned by a landlord who had large estates in that part of the country, but it was worked by a company who used it as a stock farm largely, their objects being not only to pay expenses, but also to carry out certain experiments in breeding, in order to improve the breed of dairy cattle. Superintendent Tuxon, the able manager of the place, was a man of established reputation as a farm manager.

While they also had a dairy there, it was not the chief feature, but was simply coördinate with breeding of stock and the production of grain crops. They kept 150 head of cows on the place. These remained tied in the stable all winter. I did not see this herd, for the reason that there was a "foot-and-mouth-disease" scare in that part of the country and no stranger was admitted to the barn; but Superintendent Tuxon informed me that the cattle were all of the red Danish breed and that they were all superior animals. Their management was of interest because it varied somewhat from the common custom and may be said to stand out as the best example of the management of dairy cattle to be found in the country. The cows were classified in the barn as follows: All those which were in full flow of milk; all those which had passed the period of full flow but still gave milk; all dry cows; and, lastly, all barren cows, each class standing by itself in a different part of the same barn. The feeding of these varied, and this was the main reason for their classification. Cows in full flow of milk got their first feed at 4 o'clock in the morning, consisting of 6 pounds of hay, and they were milked while eating this, between 4 and 6 a. m. At 6.30 a. m. each cow received 4½ pounds of grain, consisting of 1½ pounds of oil-meal (which was made up of one-half pound rape cake, one-half pound sunflower cake, and one-half pound palm cake), 2 pounds barley and oats mixed and ground together, and 1 pound bran. Immediately after this, each cow was given 15 pounds of whole mangels, and next they got a feed of barley straw.

Water stood before them at all times, in a little basin between each two cows, so that both drank out of the same basin. By a self-regulating valve in the supply pipe the water stood at the same height in these basins at all times. This very handy arrangement cost twelve crowns, or a trifle more than $3 per head to put up. At 1 p. m. the afternoon feeding began, which was simply a repetition of that of the forenoon.

All other cows in the barn, not in full milk, got hay, straw, and mangels as these, but they were fed different amounts of grain, according to their condition. The strictest attention was paid to cleanliness. The barn was cleaned and swept twice daily, and all the cattle were bedded twice daily. Superintendent Tuxon believed that not only the barn should be kept clean, but that it paid to keep the skins of the animals scrupulously clean. To this end he employed a man who spent his entire time currying the cattle; he went over the entire herd with currycomb and brush twice daily. One man did all of the cleaning of the stable, and another curried the cattle, while a third attended to the feeding. The temperature of the barn was kept, as nearly as possible, at 60° F. for the cows and 55° F. for the calves. No artificial heating apparatus was used, but the barn was a substantial stone structure with perfect ventilation and provision against drafts, so that it was possible to maintain this temperature even in very cold weather. None of the cows were let out of their stalls during the entire winter. The summer management was equally exacting. The cattle were put on grass about the 15th of May and remained out of doors until about the 10th of October. During the greater part of this time they were tethered in the field, each cow being secured to a stick driven in the ground, and allowed the freedom afforded by a 20-foot rope. The whole herd was thus staked out in the pasture, beginning on one side and gradually moving over to the other side. This is, doubtless, the most economical way of utilizing the pasture. Each cow was given some 3 or 4 feet of fresh pasture at each change; the grass was thus eaten up clean, and nothing was wasted by being tramped down or dirtied by the herd. This method of pasturing is in very common use on the smaller farms and also on many of the larger ones, as in this instance. The entire herd was changed five times a day at equal intervals, all the work being done by one man. The watering was attended to by another man, who, with a horse and cart, hauled the water to tubs placed between each two cows. These tubs were moved forward once in three or four days, as occasion required. All the cows giving milk were blanketed with light cotton blankets during the summer to keep the flies off, and, in addition to the pasture, they were fed a little grain daily, for the most part bran, and not to exceed 3 pounds per cow per day.

The management of the calves is also worthy of note. As soon as the calf is dropped, it is put in a small pen by itself, and within a couple of days it is injected with tuberculine to test whether or not it is affected with tuberculosis. If there is a reaction from this injection, shown by a rising temperature, then it is slaughtered at once, as this is a sure sign that it is affected; but if there is no reaction, it is spared. Then the healthy calves are put together by twos until they are 2 months old. Then four are put together in the same pen, and when the weather begins to get milder in spring they have access to a little open run in the yard. In May, when the cows are let out, all the calves are again injected with tuberculine to learn whether any of them have been infected during the winter. All which show a rise of temperature by this test are killed at once, and those which are healthy are allowed to run together without restriction as to number.

The object is to raise a herd which shall be entirely free from tuberculosis. It is admitted that at present a large percentage of the cattle in the country are affected by this disease. It is impracticable to kill all of the affected cows at once, as the loss would be too great, but by this method of weeding out infected calves the country will eventually be clear of this curse, and the object of the company, under whose auspices these experiments are carried out, is to ascertain what means can best be adopted so as to be at once effective and attended with the least loss. As to the value of tuberculine, Prof. Koch's great discovery, I was assured that in no instance had the slightest sign of the disease been found in animals which did not show a rise of temperature as a result of the injection, and, on the other hand, the germs of disease had, in every instance, been found in animals where this rise in temperature took place.

During the first summer the calves run together in a pasture to themselves. In the fall, when they are taken in, they are put, fifteen together, in a large pen and allowed to go loose. The following summer they are tethered in the same manner as the cows. The feeding of the calves is done with equal care and system. Each calf gets 300 pounds of whole milk and 2,000 pounds of skim milk up to the age of 5 months, and after that age they get no milk. It is divided about as follows: Until three weeks old all are fed the whole milk, the quantity being proportioned to the age of the calf. At 3 weeks old a little skim milk is added to the whole milk and the quantity of skim milk is then gradually increased during the next two or three weeks until, at 6 weeks old, the whole milk is entirely withdrawn. The maximum amount which is allowed in one day is 16 pounds of whole milk or 20 pounds of skim milk. All the milk is boiled and then cooled to a temperature at which the calves can drink it.

The grain feed begins at 2 months of age. They then get a small quantity of a mixture consisting of equal parts of bran and linseed meal, and this is gradually increased up to 1½ to 2 pounds per day, each, and in addition to this they always have hay before them. When the skim milk is withdrawn they are given mangels instead until they are put on pasture, and during the entire summer, while on pasture, each gets 1½ to 2 pounds of grain daily. During the following winter each gets 40 pounds of mangels, 10 pounds of hay, and 2 pounds of grain (bran and linseed cake) daily.

The heifers are bred when 15 months old and hence drop their first calves at 2 years old. During the second summer they are together as stated, but without any grain. The calves are dropped from September to February. The following is the average weight of the cattle at the ages given: Calves average the first of May about 330 pounds; the first of November, about 525 pounds; at 1½ years, about 700 pounds; at 2 years, about 825 pounds, and at 3 years, about 924 pounds. The heifers get 4 pounds of grain daily, in the fall, from the time they are put in the barn until they calve, and after calving they are treated in the same manner as cows. All cows in the herd which are not in calf are tried by a teaser every day, and if they show signs of heat, are bred to one of the fine bulls. The herd remains tied on pasture until about the middle of September, when they are turned loose on the stubble fields, these having been cleared of grain by that time.

At the time of my visit, in the beginning of February, the cows gave about 2,200 pounds of milk per day. Of this about 100 pounds was required for the young calves and the rest was set and skimmed. In this dairy no separator was used. It was run on the old plan of setting the milk in ice water and in the flat iron pans already described. The evening milk was set in the deep milk cans in ice water and the morning milk in the shallow iron pans. The milk stood from twenty-four to thirty-six hours before it was skimmed and then it was skimmed twice. The first skimming took place in the morning, when the morning milk had stood twenty-four hours and the evening milk twelve hours, and the second skimming in the evening when the evening milk had stood twenty-four hours and the morning milk thirty-six hours. In summer the iron pans were not used, all the milk being set in ice water. The cream was sterilized, not by means of a sterilizing apparatus, but by being heated to 170° F. in hot water. The water stood in a vat and was heated by steam formed in a little boiler set up for the purpose of providing hot water and steam to aid in cleaning the utensils, but not for the production of power. The cream, which had been put in deep cans, was heated by inserting the cans in this vat of hot water, the contents of each can being gently agitated all the while. When the thermometer indicated that the desired temperature was reached, the cream can was at once removed and immersed in a basin of ice water, where it was cooled to about 45° F. The dairy was in charge of an able dairywoman, and all the help in the dairy consisted of pupils who worked for their board, and neither gave nor received remuneration. Artificial cream ferment from the laboratory of Blauenfeldt & Tvede was used. The cream was warmed to 70° F. before the addition of the ferment, and at this temperature was set in the cream barrels, where it remained for twenty-eight hours in winter, falling in that time to about 60° F., at which temperature it was churned.

The churn was worked by horse power and the butter came in the same time as in the other dairies I visited where steam power was used. It required, at that time of year, 29 to 30 pounds of milk to produce a pound of butter. The butter was worked three times, in each case by hand; first, for the removal of the buttermilk, immediately after which 5 per cent of salt was added; then it was allowed to harden and the salt to melt for one hour, when it got the second working, the object being, this time, to mix the salt thoroughly; the third working took place two hours after the second.

A fine quality of skim-milk cheese was made at this dairy. The process was, briefly, as follows: The milk was warmed to 95° F. and at this temperature was added 8 per cent of buttermilk and the necessary quantity of rennet, according to its strength. If color was used it was also added then. It then stood untouched for twenty minutes while the rennet did its work. The curd was next cut and then stirred for fifty-five minutes. If the temperature had fallen during that time, it was warmed up to 96° F. by admitting steam under the vat. Half the whey was then drawn off. It was next stirred for fifteen minutes, when the remaining whey was drawn off and the curd was worked by hand. One-fourth of a pound of salt was then added for every 100 pounds of milk. The curd was then put into forms and given half pressure. At the end of an hour it was turned and replaced under the press, and two hours later it was turned again. Full pressure was then applied and it stood undisturbed until evening, when it was turned once more and a fresh cloth wrapped about it and it was again put under the press. Next morning it was taken from the cheese cup and put in strong brine, where it remained for two days; it was then put in the cheese room where a temperature of 52° to 55° F. was maintained, and there all the cheeses were daily turned and rubbed with salt or strong brine once a week. This continued for three months.

The rotation followed on this farm was as follows: First year, fallow; second year, rye; third year, barley; fourth year, one-fourth roots and three-fourths annual grass; fifth year, oats; sixth year, clover; and seventh year, one-half mixed barley and oats, and the other half in grass from the previous year's seeding. On a small portion of the farm a four-years' rotation was followed, being first year, rye; second year, roots; third year, barley; and fourth year, grass. The grass was sown with the oats and barley, respectively, in rotation. The yield of hay was about two tons to the acre. For the annual grass they used a mixture of oat grass, English rai grass, yellow medick, and sometimes a little bromus arvenses.

For the two years' grass crop in the seven-year rotation they used red clover, orchard grass, English rai grass, and meadow fescue. The average yield of rye was 50 bushels to the acre; of barley, 45 bushels; of oats, 60 bushels to the acre; and the yield of roots went as high as 24 tons to the acre. I append a statement of the receipts from the dairy, which Superintendent Tuxon kindly permitted me to draw from his books.

Statement of the products of Thurebylille Dairy and their values for the years named.

[Year reckoned from May 1 to April 30; weights in pounds avoirdupois.]

	1886-'87.	1887-'88.	1888-'89.	1889-'90.	1890-'91.	1891-'92.
Number of cows giving milk.............	135	129	127	123	127	130
Yield of milk......pounds avoirdupois..	726,752	771,810	746,447	738,133	766,286	772,275
Average yield of milk per cow.....do...	5,383	5,982	5,877	6,000	6,033	5,940
Average yield of butter per cow...do...	183.5	207.6	204.4	198.9	196.2	203.2
Butter sold per cow (inclusive of household consumption) pounds avoirdupois.	182.1	205.9	203.3	191.9	189.7	199.8
Butter value of sweet milk used on farm per cow.......... pounds avoirdupois..	6.53	4.8	5.8	8.1	15	5
Produced green cheese per cow.....do...	233.9	289.7	253.1	232.8	246.7	266.9
Produced ripe cheese per cow......do...	195.5	245	212.6	208	220.1	238.1
Live weight of swine sold per cow..do...	185.7	214.5	245.7	240.6	231	236.1
Shrink in butter..............per cent..	.8	.8	.4	3.1	3.4	1.9
Milk required to make 1 pound butter ....pounds..	28.5	28.2	28	·29.5	29.2	28.9
Skim milk required per pound green cheese............................pounds..	13.5	13.4	13.3	13.4	13.1	13.2
Shrink in cheese ....per cent..	16.4	12.2	16	10.7	10.8	10.8
Price of butter per pound avoirdupois:						
In summer ....cents..	21.6	22.8	21.5	22.9	21.6	22.3
In winter........................do...	25.02	25	25	25.02	27	27
Price per pound avoirdupois of skim-milk cheese.........................cents..	3.15	4.72	4.7	3.97	5.2	5.62
Price per pound of swine (live weight avoirdupois)....................cents..	6.27	5.88	6.41	6.97	7.38	7.63
Receipts from each pound of skim milk:						
In cheese ....cents..	.2	.31	.29	.26	.35	.42
In whey........................do...	.098	.11	.11	.15	.19	.198
Total receipts per pound of skim milk .... cents..	.298	.42	.4	.41	.54	.618
Receipts from each pound sweet milk .... cents..	1.08	1.10	1.2	1.15	1.3	1.30
Gross receipts per cow..................	$58.14	$71.51	$79.54	$69.51	$77.89	$81.21

VALDEMAR CASTLE.

This old castle is situated on the small island called Tosinge, which lies close to the Isle of Funen. The farm consisted of 630 acres. On this area were kept, at the time of my visit, 120 dairy cows, about half of which were in milk and the other half dry. They were stabled in an excellent barn, the plan of which may be seen in the accompanying illustration (Figs. 20 and 21), which I give as a sample of the barns that are generally found on the large farms.

The barn was built of brick with stone foundation, and was one story high, with a high roof. It was entirely fireproof. The ceiling was of brick laid on iron arches, and the only openings from the inside were those necessary to admit hay and bedding, which were stored under the roof. At intervals there were brick flues for ventilators, which ran to the crest of the roof, and the roof itself was of tiles. There was no wood in the interior of the structure except the door and window frames. There were no partitions between the stalls, and all the posts were of iron.

Fig. 21 shows a plan of the barn; *a* represents the rows of stalls, and *b* the feed alley between the stalls. The floor of this alley was raised a foot and a half above the floor of the stalls. At both ends of

FIG. 20.—Side view of cattle barn at Valdemar castle.

the barn were loose boxes marked *c*, inclosed with an iron fence. These were, for the most part, used for calves; *m* represents the mangers, which were made of curved tiles laid in cement so that they were perfectly water-tight, and the cattle were watered in these mangers twice daily. At one end of the barn were three feed-bins indicated by *f*, and in the middle of the barn was a short wing which contained the herdsman's room *h*, and a large room for mangels, *n*. The floor of the barn, except the feed alley, was a pavement of squared stones nicely

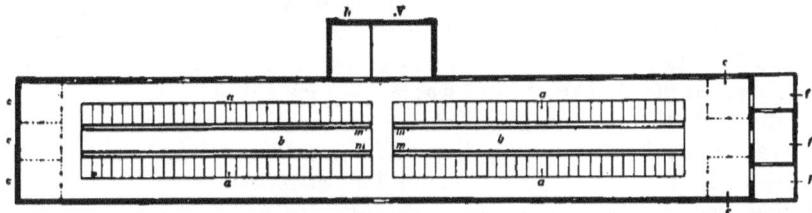

FIG. 21.—Ground plan of cattle barn at Valdemar castle.

fitted together, and provision was made for the drainage of the liquid manure into large cisterns. I did not learn what the cost of this barn was, but it must have been considerable. On the other hand, it was of such a substantial nature that it will last for centuries.

The cows were fed as follows: At 5 a. m. they were fed straw, and the milking took place while this was being eaten; at 7 a. m. each cow got 10 pounds of mangels, and immediately after 5 pounds of grain, consisting of the following mixture: One pound of cocoanut cake, 2 pounds of sunflower cake, 2 pounds of bran, 3 pounds of oats, and 2 pounds of barley, the two latter being ground together. After this was eaten they were watered. Next they got a feed of straw or of chaff. At 12 m. they got a small feed of hay. At 1 p. m. the afternoon feeding began with 10 pounds of roots, then half of the above mixture of grain, and then water. Next straw, and again a feed of straw at 7 p. m. The cows were fine specimens of the red Danish breed. The average yield of milk per cow for the year was 4,950 pounds avoirdupois, including barren cows and heifers. Some of the cows were large milkers, one of them yielding 68 pounds per day.

The milk is handled as follows, according to the statement of the chief dairymaid:

The evening milk is set in tall 50-pound cans, and these are sunk in ice water. These cans are hand skimmed in the morning, and the skim milk is run through the separator, which still produces 4 pounds of cream to 100 pounds of milk. When the milk has been skimmed in this way all the cream is sterilized by being heated to 167° F. This is accomplished by immersing the cream cans in hot water, the sterilizing apparatus being out of order. It is next cooled to about 40° F., at which temperature it remains for a couple of hours. It is then heated again to 78° F., and at this temperature the ferment is added. The ferment in this case consists of sour cream saved from the morning's churning, 20 per cent of this sour cream being added. It then stands in the cream barrel, in a protected place, for eighteen hours, or from noon one day to 6 a. m. the next, when it is churned.

The dairymaid held that this cream ferment had given her better results than any other methods she had tried. In summer she set the cream to sour at only 60° F., but she then added a greater quantity of sour cream, and the same results were obtained. She churned the cream in winter at from 59° to 62° F. and washed the utensils with clean water at 56° F. The butter came, usually, in twenty-five minutes. The revolving dasher in the churn made 140 revolutions per minute. In summer the churning temperature was 52° F. The butter she made was of first quality, and always brought about $1.35 per 100 pounds over the highest quotation at the exchange in Copenhagen. She added 4½ per cent of salt in winter and 6 per cent in summer, and she assured me that the butter would keep for half a year.

She took the following precautions in packing butter: First, the barrel was soaked for twenty-four hours in cold water and next it was filled with brine, which remained in it for twenty-four hours. Then the inside was thoroughly rubbed with salt. In the meantime paraffin paper was prepared by soaking in brine for several hours, and lastly in saltpeter for a half hour, and the barrel was then lined with this; finally a half inch of salt was put on the bottom of the barrel. The butter was then firmly packed in, the top covered with a sheet of paraffin paper, on top of this half an inch of salt, and then the head was put on. The barrels thus packed were kept in a cool room adjoining the ice house until they were shipped, and each barrel was rolled about for some time once a week in order to prevent the brine from settling too much in one place.

The skim milk was sterilized before it was fed to the calves, and cheese was made from what was left after feeding the calves and taking out what was required for the household. It required 22 pounds of milk to make a pound of butter in summer and fall and 25 pounds in winter.

FAAREVEILE FARM.

This farm is situated on the island of Langeland (Longland). I paid a flying visit to it because, in my travels about the country, I had heard the dairy products from this place highly spoken of, and I even heard of the butter from this farm while among the butter dealers in London. My time, however, was so limited that I could only interview the dairy manager, but the establishment owed its reputation chiefly to his skill. He was a young man by the name of Neilsen Holm, who had studied dairying in the best establishments of the country. The following notes were taken from his statements:

There were 250 cows on the farm, and of these 200 were in milk at the time of my visit. The stalls were cleaned in the morning from 3 to 4:30 a. m., and immediately after this the cows were milked. The first feed was given at 7 a. m. and consisted of half a bushel of whole mangels. When these were eaten they were fed grain consisting of 2 pounds of barley and oats ground together, 2 pounds of bran, and 1 pound of rape-seed cake; they were next watered at about 8 a. m., the water being run into the manger in front of them. After the water they got 4 pounds of hay per head, and when this was eaten a liberal feed of barley straw. They were then bedded down, the doors were closed and the stable kept as quiet as possible for the remainder of the forenoon. At 1 p. m. the feeding began again with another half bushel of whole mangels and then 5 pounds of grain of the same mixture as above; next water, hay, and straw in succession as in the forenoon. The stable was again cleaned from 3 to 4:30 p. m. and the milking took place immediately after; finally a feed of straw was given about 7 in the evening.

The herd, as a whole, was first class. Many of the cows gave as much as 6,600 pounds avoirdupois of milk per year. He selected calves intended to be raised to fill places in the herd only from the best cows. Good cows were bought wherever they could be found. The cows were tested by the so-called "trial-milkings," which occurred twice a month. It consists in weighing the milk from each cow separately, at both milkings, on fixed dates, and from this the yield is estimated. The cows were not named but numbered, each being known by her number only. Special attention was also given to the breeding of bulls on this farm, and the few bull calves which, in point of pedigree and individual merits, were considered good enough to raise, sold for high prices. The milk was run through a De Laval "Alpha" separator as soon as it reached the dairy, at a temperature of 86° F., and the cream was at once put in ice water and cooled to 50° F. in the winter, and in summer to 45° F., and was kept at this until time to sour it. It was then warmed to 77° F. and at 10 a. m. put in the cream barrel at this temperature and 5 per cent of ferment added.

The ferment was made thus: Healthy cows were selected which had been in milk about six weeks. This milk was put in ice water as soon as it arrived at the dairy and cooled to 40° F. Here it remained five hours, and whatever cream rose in that time was skimmed off. The skim milk was then warmed to 100° F. and immediately put aside in large earthenware jars, and these, in winter, kept in a box lined with a hay mattress to keep out the cold. Put away thus at 11 a. m. it remained until the next morning at 8 a. m., when the jars are opened and the upper 2 inches skimmed off to avoid contamination from injurious bacteria which might have found lodging on the surface. The milk, which had become sour, was then thoroughly mixed by being violently stirred and then cooled while exposed to fresh air to 50° or 54° F., and finally, at 10 a. m., it was added to the cream in the cream barrels. Occasionally buttermilk was used as a ferment, but, as a rule, this skim milk ferment was prepared and used daily. After the ferment was added the cream stood from 10 a. m. until 5 a. m. the next morning, but was stirred four times during the day. At 5 a. m. it was transferred to tall cans which were sunk in ice water until the cream showed a temperature of 12° R. (59 F.), at which temperature it was churned in winter. From the 200 cows in milk 330 pounds of cream was obtained daily. The churn was run by steam, the dasher making 140 revolutions per minute, and butter came in from 30 to 35 minutes. The butter received three workings on the machine; after the first working it was weighed and 4 per cent of salt was added; one-half hour later it was worked again, and two to two and a half hours later it received the final working. It was then packed in barrels in the same manner as has already been described. It took 26 pounds of milk to make a pound of butter. The butter was sold by contract to one dealer for the whole year, the agreement being to pay about $26 per 100 pounds of butter; but for the ensuing year's contract I was informed the price would be raised to about $30 per 100 pounds. The butter was strictly a first-quality article.

JULESBERG FARM.

I made a brief visit to a large farm of that name situated a short distance from the city of Nyborg. There were 130 cows on the place, but, in addition to the milk from these, milk was bought from some of the smaller farms in the neighborhood, so that the total amount handled was nearly 5,000 pounds daily. The creamery was of the improved type, equipped with all the machinery demanded by the most advanced methods. This milk produced about 195 pounds of butter daily. All the cream was pasteurized before it was fermented. The ferment used was usually produced on the place, from skim milk, in the manner already described, but they also used pure cultures when it was thought advantageous to do so. The dairy was in charge of a woman, who informed me that she churned at 57° F. during the winter, and that the cream was set to sour at from 68° to 72° F., according to the weather, and she used 4½ per cent salt to the butter.

The cows on the farm were fed as follows: They were milked between 4 and 6.30 a. m. This done they got their first feed, which consisted of 4 pounds of a mixture made up of one-half part each of rape-seed cake and cotton-seed cake, and one part each of bran and barley and oats ground together. After this they got a feed of hay, then water, and next straw. This completed the feeding for the forenoon. At 1 p. m. it began again with grain, as above, then 15 pounds of sliced mangels, then two feeds of straw in succession. Of the 130 cows on the place 92 of all ages were in milk, and these gave 1,850 pounds of milk daily, and the best cow gave at that time 48 pounds of milk daily.

In summer the cows were tethered in the pasture. The milking was done by women, each of whom milked 20 cows in two and one-half hours. I found on this farm some 25 or 30 head of steers which were being fattened. They were fed entirely on oil cake and mangels. Each steer got 5 pounds of rape-seed cake daily and all the mangels he would eat, but no water, the mangels supplying water enough for the needs of the system. This mode of fattening is so unusual that I can not forbear to mention it here. The feed-master assured me that they gained about 3 pounds daily, per head, under this treatment. They were of the ordinary dairy breed of the country, and were tied up in the stable, never being let out.

BRAHETROLLEBORG.

This is the country seat of Count Reventlow. The home farm of the estate comprised about 660 acres, about 100 acres of which were in permanent meadow and the rest under culture. The herd consisted of 161 cows and 3 bulls, and 22 horses were used to work the farm. The cattle got their first feed at 4 o'clock in the morning and while they ate this the milking took place. The second feed was given at 6:30 in the morning, consisting of three pounds of barley and oats ground together, 2 pounds of bran, 1 pound of rape-seed cake and one pound of palm cake. They were next watered in the mangers, after which they got a feed of chaff, and when this was eaten they had a feed of oat or barley straw, which completed the feeding for the forenoon. At 1 p. m. they were again given grain, water, chaff, and hay in succession, and finally a feed of straw in the evening. The milking began at 4 a. m., the stable being cleaned before milking. The bulls had each 4 pounds of grain per day and straw and hay, as the cows. No roots were fed upon this place. At the time of my visit 82 cows were in milk, which yielded about 1,450 pounds milk per day. They still used the old system of setting the milk in cold water, where it stood twenty-four hours before it was skimmed. The cream was then warmed to 68° F. and soured by the use of buttermilk from last churning. Pure culture cream ferment was used when necessary. The cream stood 24 hours after the buttermilk was added. They also occasionally made fresh ferment from skim milk in the manner already described elsewhere. From the amount of milk given they obtained 57 pounds of butter daily. The butter was worked three times, four per cent of salt being added at the first working. The price realized from the sale of the butter was somewhat less than that of some of the other places I have noted.

Cheese was made from the skim milk by the following process: The milk was warmed to 95° F. in winter and 92° in summer, and prepared rennet added when the temperature was reached. It then stood undisturbed for three-quarters of an hour, when the curd was cut and slowly stirred for twenty minutes, until the whey became clear. It then rested for ten minutes, after which it was again stirred a little and when the whey was perfectly clear it was drawn off and the curd pressed with the hands in the cheese vat, to work off the whey. Salt and caraway seed were then added. This completed, it was transferred to the cheese cups and put under the press, the pressure being light at first. At the end of an hour the cheese was turned in the cups and replaced under the press, where it remained until next morning, but it was turned twice more in the meantime. On being removed from the press the cheeses were put in strong brine, where they remained for twenty-four hours, and they were then put in the cheese room, where the temperature was kept at about 54° F. Here they were turned daily and each time wiped with a dry cloth, this process being continued until they were thoroughly dry. They were kept for at least two months and sometimes much longer, according to the market. The dairy was in charge of a superintendent, to whom I am indebted for these facts. He stated, further, that he made a pound of green cheese from 11 pounds of milk, and that his cheese shrank 15 per cent in weight in the process of drying.

On this farm were 20 head of high-grade shorthorn heifers, 3 and 4 years old, being fattened for market. They were in extra fine condition and estimated to average about 1,600 pounds in weight. They were tied up in the barn, as the dairy cows, and were never let out, being fed and watered in the stalls. They had been on good pasture without grain during the summer and when put in the stable in the fall they were fed hay and straw, turnips and kohlrabi, all they would eat, but no grain. This treatment was continued for one month, then 2 pounds of linseed cake was added to the ration. During the next month this was increased to 6 pounds per head, and in addition some of the largest got 2 pounds of barley and oats.

SMALL DAIRY FARMS.

In the following account I shall briefly describe the processes, both in the dairy and in the cultivation of the soil, which are followed on the small Danish farms. Possibly they may furnish hints of greater usefulness to the majority of farmers in the United States than do those of the large farms. There are but few farms in this country where one hundred or even fifty dairy cows are kept, and fewer still where the dairy is fully equipped with all the modern machinery. Here the farm dairy is on a small scale, and as to material and practical methods of work, it therefore comes nearer the small Danish farms.

FARM OF MADAME NIELSEN.

One of the first of this class of farms which it was my privilege to visit is situated an hour's ride on the railway from Copenhagen and belongs to Madame Nielsen, who named it Havarthigaard. This lady is known outside of Denmark for her dairy products. For nearly thirty-five years she has been a close student of dairying, both at home and abroad, having made several trips to various European countries

FIG. 22.—Perspective of Madame Nielsen's buildings.

in order to study their methods and obtain points which she could apply to her own practice. She has thus visited England, Holland, Switzerland, Norway, and France at various times. She has met with signal success. She supplies the butter for the table of the King and Queen, a few pounds being sent to the palace by express every morning from her house. In cheese-making she is equally successful. Her cheese sells for many times the price obtained for ordinary cheese. She even sends cheese to the Emperor of Russia, who learned to appreciate her dairy products on his visits to Copenhagen. He usually carries home a supply when returning from one of these visits, and consignments are occasionally sent to the palace in St. Petersburg.

Most of her produce, both butter and cheese, is sold to special high-class customers, and the surplus not sold in this manner is disposed of in a little shop in the exhibition building in Copenhagen, where she herself waits upon customers every afternoon. She is famous not only as a practical dairywoman but as a teacher of darying as well. She informed me that she had instructed no fewer than 1,000 pupils in her dairy methods. It is quite the thing for young persons of both sexes, who have completed their course in dairying elsewhere, to finish up with a few weeks or a few months with Madame Nielsen, and many of the chief dairywomen that I met elsewhere had, at some time or other, been at her establishment. She charges a good round fee of them, usually about $27, whether they stay for a long or short time, and while there, by the terms of the agreement, they do the work in the dairy of whatever kind. At the time of my visit, in January, there were four young ladies studying dairying, and I was informed that by the first of March two more were to come.

The farm on which she has developed this famous little dairy is 166 acres in extent. The farm management is in the hands of her husband and son-in-law, who, with his wife, lives with them; but the management of the dairy cows and of the dairy is all under her own supervision. I obtained an introduction to this lady through Prof. Segelcke, and by special arrangement it was agreed that I should visit her place, stay over night, so as to be on hand early in the morning, when I might have the privilege of learning what I could of what was going on about me.

At the time of my visit she had 19 cows giving milk, the total number in the herd being between 25 and 30 cows. The milking began at 4:30 in the morning and was done by the pupils. The cows were not fed until 6:30, when they got a feed of 3 pounds of grain, consisting of a mixture of bran, barley, and oats ground together in equal quantities, and three-fourths of a pound of rape-seed cake, which was soaked in water for twenty-four hours previously and mixed with the grain. In half to three-fourths of an hour each cow had three-fourths of a bushel of mangels. At 8 a. m. they received a big feed of barley straw or oat straw, the surplus not eaten being used for bedding. At 11 a. m. they were watered in the manger, after which they had a feed of hay, all they could eat. This finished the feeding for the forenoon. They were not fed again until 5 p. m., when they had the same amount of grain as above and after that all the straw they could eat and later water, but no mangels or hay was given them in the afternoon.

In the beginning of May the cows are put on pasture for two or three weeks, but as soon as the grass gets tall enough to cut they are again stabled and stall-fed on green fodder until after harvest, when they are again let out for five or six weeks. They are not tethered, as is the usual custom, but run loose when they are out. The cows were of the red Danish breed, and there were several excellent animals among them. Ten or twelve heifer calves are raised every year, those not wanted to take the place of older cows being sold.

The calves are fed during the first two weeks of their lives on whole milk; but at the end of this time skim milk is mixed with the whole milk, gradually increasing the skim milk until they get no whole milk at all, and when about ten weeks old the skim milk is partly substituted by whey and bran. This, with hay and straw in winter and grass in the summer, forms the diet of the calves. The following winter they get roots in addition to hay and straw and a little grain. The heifers are bred when fifteen months old so as to drop the first calf when two years of age. Twice a month there is a trial milking, when the milk from each cow is weighed separately, but for the rest of the time all the milk is weighed together.

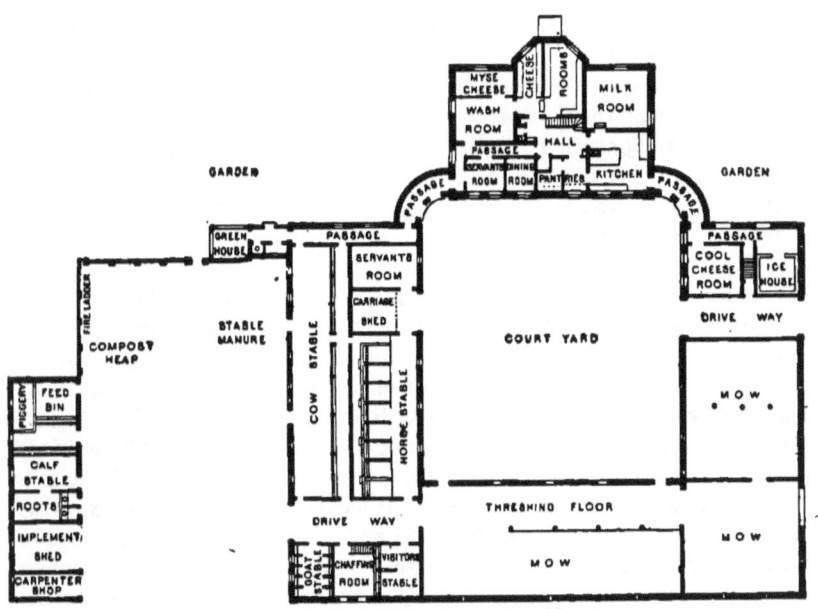

FIG. 23.—Madame Nielsen's buildings—plan of basement.

Madame Nielsen's dairy, I found, was small and by no means of a style which is unattainable by American farmers. It was all in the basement (Fig. 23) under the dwelling house. The milk was set in tall cylindrical cans, and these sunk in ice water, there being several basins constructed of brick laid in cement for the purpose of holding this ice water. The kitchen adjoined the milk-room, and most of the work in buttter and cheese making was done in the kitchen. The milk stood twenty-four hours before it was skimmed. As only about 300 pounds of milk were handled per day during the winter, no separator was needed, nor was any sterilizing apparatus used; all the work was done in the good old-fashioned way and with the best results. The utmost cleanliness was apparent everywhere. All the utensils were scoured and scrubbed until they fairly shone. The floors were clean. Care was used in the ventilation to let in all the fresh air possible and still maintain the desired temperature, and pure water and ice were used in abundance. The cream, when skimmed from the milk, was put in an earthenware jar scrupulously clean. She used in souring the cream a ferment that she makes from skim milk. She used milk from a cow nearly fresh. This stood twelve hours and was then skimmed. It was then warmed to 100° or 105° F., and set away in a place where the temperature could be kept moderately uniform, where it remained twenty-four hours. At the end of this time it developed the proper degree of sourness, the temperature in the winter, in the meantime, having fallen to 68° or 70° F. Some 5 per cent of this prepared ferment was added to the cream about the middle of the forenoon, the cream being first warmed to 75° F. The cream jar was packed in a box lined with a hay mattress, in order to prevent cooling too rapidly. In the course of the day the cream was stirred several times and in the evening it began to thicken. It was then removed from the hay box and kept at a somewhat cooler temperature over night, and at 5 o'clock the following morning the churn was started. The churning temperature varies greatly with the season and the condition. It may range from 55° to 75° F.

When I was there the cream was warmed to 61° F. The churning was done by hand by the side of the kitchen stove in a little churn of the usual pattern of the country, the revolving dasher being turned by a crank and the power supplied by the muscular arms of one of the young lady pupils. On the sign of formation of butter the churning proceeded more slowly, and when the granules were as large as pin heads the churn was washed down with water at about 50° F. Madame Nielsen herself takes the butter out of the churn and works it in an old-fashioned wooden butter trough, but she never touches it with her hands. It was worked three times at brief intervals. At the second working, the buttermilk having been removed at the first working, 4 per cent of salt was added, and immediately after the third working it was packed in china crocks for transmission by express to the several special customers.

The method of souring the cream here described was not her invariable practice, however. Sometimes she would warm the cream in an enameled kettle to 84° F., after which she would add 5 per cent of buttermilk from the last churning. This would stand for three or four hours in the cream jar until the temperature of the cream had fallen to 66° or 68° F., when it was transferred to the hay-lined box to maintain this temperature as nearly as possible, and it remained there until bedtime, when it had begun to thicken. If the box should then afford too much warmth the jar was taken out and set on the floor or in water, according to circumstances, until morning. She attached special importance to the following points:

(1) That the churning temperature was properly adjusted to the season

and the quality of the cream, as this might be affected by the feed of the cows, or the number of fresh cows in the herd, and other varying conditions; (2) that the fermentation of the cream began at a relatively high degree of warmth; (3) that the temperature of the cream was gradually reduced during the time that the ferment was acting; and (4) that the cream thus treated should stand for some time (over night) at the temperature of about 50° F. before it was churned. In the morning the cream was warmed to the proper temperature for churning by setting the cream jar in warm water. By this method she claimed to be able always to produce the finest quality of butter. She had not, as yet, found it necessary to use the pure cultures in the fermentation of her cream.

Simultaneously with the churning, preparations were made for the making of cheese. She made three kinds of cheese while I was there, sweet-milk cheese, Camembert cheese, and Myse cheese, and occasionally she made some half dozen other kinds of cheese, in all of which she was very expert. The sweet-milk cheese was begun first. As soon as the milk was received from the barn and it had been weighed and strained, it was warmed to 88° F. by setting the cans of milk in kettles of warm water on the stove. To a hundred pounds of sweet milk she added 64 pounds of skim milk, so it was not strictly a full-cream cheese. When the milk had reached the temperature of 88° F. the rennet was added.

She used rennet at the rate of two one-hundredths of a pound of the fluid extract to 100 pounds of milk. A little buttermilk was added along with the rennet. It was then allowed to stand undisturbed for twenty-five minutes, at the end of which time it had coagulated, when it was cut with a curd knife. After this it was gently stirred to clear the whey, and if the temperature had fallen during the interval it was warmed a little during the process of stirring. When the curd had settled to the bottom the whey was drawn off and the lump of curd quartered and the outside turned into the middle of the vat in order, as she stated, to drain it equally and make it of the same consistency throughout; otherwise it would have been firmer in the middle. When the whey had drained off, the curd was broken into large pieces by hand and these were packed in the cheese cup with layers of caraway seed. No salt was added, as it gets enough of that substance during the process of curing.

The form of the cheese cup should be mentioned. It could be enlarged by the addition of rings, and as the cheese was compressed and required less room these rings were removed. When the cup was filled it was placed under the cheese press, but only a very light pressure was applied. It was put in press at 9 a. m. usually, and at 9:30 the cheese was turned and pricked through and through with a prong. It was again turned at 11 and again soon after noon, at 4 p. m., and at 9 p. m., but remained in the press until the following morning. It was then removed from the cup, rubbed with salt and put in a wooden bowl with a rounded bottom, where it stood for some time in order that the sharp edges might be removed and the cheese take a rounded shape. It was rubbed with salt and turned in this bowl three times a day for four days; then it was put in the cheese room and rubbed with salt once a day. This was continued for six weeks; it was then changed to another room of a slightly cooler temperature and rubbed with brine once every other day, which process was continued until the cheese was sold. She attached great importance to this frequent rubbing with salt. It not only makes the rind soft and practically prevents the formation of any rind whatever, but she called my attention to the fact that her cheese was covered with a fatty layer, which she said was drawn out by the salt, and which effectually prevented the access of air to the interior of the cheese. It is a well-known fact that the best cheese is cured in the absence of air in the interior. She made, at that time of the year, only one cheese of 16 pounds' weight per day. After about three months' curing, or longer, the cheese was sold, and it brought about 25 cents per pound, when the ordinary skim-milk cheese brought but from 4 to 5 cents per pound.

Camembert cheese is a kind of specially rich cheese which she makes from whole sweet milk every morning, as soon as the milk is drawn from the cows, weighed, and strained. It was my privilege to assist in making this cheese. The process was as follows: The fresh milk, warm from the cow, was warmed to 100° F. At this temperature she added one one-hundredth pound of rennet for each 10 pounds of milk, after which it was gently stirred, and then allowed to stand for four and one-half hours, when it had coagulated to the proper degree. The cheese vat used was a large earthen jar, which was kept wrapped up and placed near the stove so as to maintain the same temperature of 100° F. until coagulation was completed. The curd was then cut into small squares, but not worked or pressed in the least. When cut sufficiently fine, curd and whey together were dipped out and put in small tin rings or molds with holes in the sides, but with neither bottom nor top. Each form, or mold, consisted of two rings, one placed on top of the other, and when thus arranged they were about 6 inches high and measured 5 inches in diameter. They rested on a strainer placed on top of a vessel, and over the strainer was laid a little mat made of clean, stiff, rye straws, single straws being tied parallel to each other. This was to drain off the whey, and the straw mats facilitated the turning of the cheese. When the cups were full they were left undisturbed for eight hours in a warm place near the stove. By the end of that time the cheese had settled so much that the upper ring or half of the mold was removed and the cheese was turned, but left in the cup over night. Next morning they were turned again and salted on one side. Three or four hours later they were again turned and salted on the other side. No pressure was applied at any time. During all this time the temperature did not fall below

78° F. After the second salting it had acquired sufficient solidity to be removed from the mold. It was then placed in a room with the temperature from 55° to 60° F., where it remained for two or three weeks, when it was placed in the cheese room with a somewhat higher temperature. It was ready for sale when two months old, and sold at 1 crown, or 27 cents, apiece and weighed three-fourths of a pound. She made about fourteen cheeses daily of this kind, from 80 pounds of milk, the total weight being 10 pounds of cheese. Some cream was sometimes added to the milk before it was curdled, if she had the cream to spare.

Myse cheese is made of the solid matter left in the whey after the water has been evaporated. It consists chiefly of milk-sugar, with most of the ash elements of the milk, and the albumen and fat not removed in cheese-making. It originated in Norway, where they use the milk of goats chiefly, which is said to produce the finest quality. But it can be made from any kind of whey, sweet milk, or skim milk, and, as a matter of fact, is so made. It therefore varies greatly in composition. Mr. Bòggild makes, on the authority of a Norwegian chemist named Werenskjold, the statement, that Norwegian Myse cheese will vary in composition as follows: Water, from 24 to 38 per cent; ash, from $5\frac{1}{2}$ to $6\frac{1}{4}$ per cent; fat, from 1 to 10 per cent; lactic acid, from $\frac{1}{10}$ to $\frac{1}{2}$ per cent; albuminoids, from $6\frac{1}{2}$ to 9 per cent, and other substances, consisting chiefly of milk sugar, from 46 to 61 per cent.

Madame Nielsen allowed nothing to go to waste. Every morning the whey, which was obtained from her sweet milk and her Camembert cheese, was made into Myse cheese and, to give it the genuine flavor, she kept half a dozen goats, whose milk also contributed to it. As soon as all the whey was collected it was divided between half a dozen enameled pots, each holding several gallons, and these were placed over the cook stove and here the whey was evaporated, being constantly kept at the boiling point while it was continuously and violently stirred. This kept all her pupils busy for a couple of hours. As the whey evaporated, so that the contents in the pot became less, it was poured into an adjoining pot until there was only one kettle over the fire. As the mass thickened the stirring increased, and finally it became so thick that it could no longer be prevented from burning, It was then put into a trough, where it was pounded and beaten with wooden clubs like potato mashers, with all the might the young ladies possessed and, when made perfectly homogeneous, it was tamped closely into a square wooden mold and put under pressure. It forms a greenish-yellow, sweetish mass, rather agreeable to the taste and very nutritious. No rennet is added, nor any flavoring whatever. It is ready to eat as soon as it comes out of the mold, but it will also keep for a couple of months. It should be kept in a covered vessel to prevent it from drying up. This cheese sold at the same price as the sweet-milk cheese. During the summer season she made also Chester cheese, Gorkonsola, Edam cheese, and other kinds.

There is a lesson to be learned from this remarkable woman. With no advantages in education or resources above those possessed by the vast majority of her sisters, she has, by devoting herself to the household arts with energy and skill, attained not only an international reputation, but has accumulated a comfortable little fortune. Fig. 22 shows a perspective of her house and barns, and Fig. 23 a plan of the same, in which the dairy rooms are pointed out.

FARM OF P. PEDERSEN.

I will next briefly describe a small place which I visited in the village of Sóllinge, on the island of Funen. The place is owned by a school teacher, Mr. P. Pedersen, who teaches school daily in addition to overseeing the work on his little farm. The property consists of 7 acres, which he described to me as a soil of ordinary quality with a clay subsoil. He has owned it since 1876. About one acre was occupied with buildings and garden; the garden was closely planted with apples, pears, cherries, and between these gooseberries, currants, and raspberries. The remaining 6 acres were divided into five lots, one-fifth being in perpetual meadow. The other four parts are cultivated as follows, in a four-year rotation: The first year, one-third of one of these quarters was in rye or wheat, one-third in some soiling crop, chiefly a mixture of vetches and oats, and one-third was given up to the production of seed of turnips, mangels, and cabbage. A second quarter of the small farm was given up to roots for the cattle, potatoes, and green peas, the latter being raised for market. Of the third quarter, two-thirds was sown in barley or a mixture of barley and oats, which was used for feed, and one-third was given up to a variety of vegetables. The last quarter was two-thirds in grass and one-third in vegetables. This rotation was followed constantly; thus, the quarter with rye and soiling crops one year was the next year planted with roots, potatoes, and green peas; the third year with barley and vegetables, and the fourth year with grass and vegetables. High manuring and thorough culture make it possible to keep four high-class dairy cows and one heifer on this very small farm.

Every particle of manure was saved. The liquid manure was collected in a cistern and applied to the grass land, to the fruit trees, and plats devoted to seed growing, and the solid manure was applied to the root crops, the soiling crops, and to the vegetables. Besides the cows he kept two brood sows and yearly fattened 8 or 10 head of swine, all from the products of this little place. But with all this live stock, which produced considerable manure, he informed me that he still bought yearly 200 pounds of kainit, 400 pounds of Thomas slag, and 200 pounds of Chile saltpeter, which were applied to the grain crops. The dairy cows were fed grain both summer and winter. The winter ration consisted of a mixture of oil cake, bran, and barley and oats ground together. The quantity given each varied with the amount of milk she produced, but the feed was not excessively heavy, usually from 8 to 10 pounds of this mixture per day, in addition to which each cow would get 40 pounds of roots, 4 pounds of hay, and 8 pounds of straw. During the summer the cows were, for the most part, fed in the stable also, but were tethered on good pasture an average of two hours daily, and in addition each cow received about 4 pounds of grain daily.

I was interested in this very intensive system of agriculture and procured detailed accounts of receipts and expenditures. During the year 1892 the five head of cattle mentioned consumed 10,788 pounds of grain feed of the mixture above mentioned, valued at 608 crowns ($166), and they also consumed roots and hay valued at 222 crowns ($64). Total expense for feed, $230, all of which, except the oil cake, was produced upon the place. The cows gave in return 30,438 pounds avoirdupois of milk, which, at the price received for milk at the coöperative dairy, was worth 1,073 crowns ($294). This left but $64 profit, but he placed a very high estimate on the feed, and the milk was valued at only factory prices. As a matter of fact, more was made from it by making it into butter and cheese at home, and the sale of a heifer brought 165 crowns ($45). The swine ate 8,845 pounds grain, together with the whey and skim milk not otherwise used, and offal from the garden, on which he put a total value of 745 crowns ($204), which seems a high valuation. The receipts were 902 crowns ($247), from seven fat swine and twenty-one sucking pigs, but not including two or three head slaughtered for home consumption. I did not receive details of the fruit, vegetables, and seed sold, which must have been no inconsiderable item. These articles would have brought still better prices if the place had been located near the city, where they could have been sold to the best advantage. But, as it is, it is a fine example of the possibilities of a small place when properly attended to.

FARM OF HANS HANSEN.

I next visited another farmer in the same neighborhood, Hans Hansen, of Sóllinge. He owns a farm of 93 acres and he had, at the time of my visit, 32 cows, 16 heifers, and 3 bulls. His cattle were of the best strain of the red Danish dairy cattle. He was, in fact, a breeder of fine dairy stock as well as a farmer. Several of his cows gave between 50 and 60 pounds of milk daily, and he got in the neighborhood of $100 apiece for promising heifers. The average milk yield of his cows had been up to 8,800 pounds per cow, young and old, yearly; but during the last two years his herd had been troubled with abortion, which had somewhat reduced the milk yield. Still, during the year 1892, his 32 cows produced 226,317 pounds of milk, avoirdupois, which was sold to the coöperative creamery, besides what was used in the household, concerning which I did not get details. This brings the average to 7,072 pounds per cow for the milk sold. His cattle are fed in the following manner: During the winter, first feed was given at 6:30 a. m., and consisted of 6 pounds of hay, and a little later three-fourths of a bushel of mangels. He used oil cake to a considerable extent, each cow getting about 6 pounds per day when in full flow, which was divided into two feeds, each feed being mixed with an equal weight of ground oats. His oil cake consists of equal parts of cotton-seed cake and sunflower cake, rape-seed cake and hemp-seed cake. After 3 pounds of this oil cake and 3 pounds of oats had been eaten the cows were watered, and then followed a feed of barley or oat straw, which finished the feeding for the forenoon. The afternoon feeding began at 3:30, this time with the roots, then grain, as above, water, and straw for the night, no hay being given in the afternoon. The cattle remained in the barn all winter without being let out once; the manger was built water-tight and the water turned into it twice a day, and what was not drunk was again drained off.

His barns were models of solidity and convenience. They were built of brick, with floors of squared stone and stalls and all auxiliaries of the most substantial nature. The drainage of the stables was well nigh perfect. Nothing was allowed to go to waste. The urine was collected in large cisterns, from which it was pumped out and hauled to the grass lands during the spring and summer, and the solid manure was kept under shelter. In summer the whole herd was tethered in the pasture, or stall-fed with soiling crops if the pasture was at all short. He practiced a seven-year rotation, as follows: First year, oats, half of which is sown to grass; second year, this half remains in grass and the other half is sown in soiling crops, which is either a mixture of vetches and oats or field peas and oats; third year, it is in rye; fourth year, three-fourths is in roots and one-fourth in barley; fifth year, oats sown with clover and grass seed; sixth year, meadow, and seventh year, pasture, which ends the rotation, the pasture being again broken up for oats. The manure is applied chiefly to the grass land and to the roots. The owner is now past middle age, but still active and energetic. By careful attention to his farm he has accumulated a fortune which enables him to present each of his several children with a comfortable farm, while he and his wife will live in comfort during their coming old age.

FARM OF CHRISTIAN RASMUSSEN.

I next visited several small farms on the island of Langeland, some of which I shall describe. In the village of Clausebólle I had a talk with a farmer named Christian Rasmussen. He owns 32 acres of land, on which he kept two horses, nine cows, several head of young cattle, besides half a dozen hogs, and a lot of poultry. His cows were of a good ordinary quality, but made no pretentions to be pure-bred stock. The nine cows averaged 6,600 pounds avoirdupois of milk per year.

The products of his dairy netted him in 1892 about $55 per cow, not counting the labor; this is very nearly equal to $500 from the cows alone. He sold pigs for about $54, and wheat for about $200. This makes a total of nearly $750 as the receipts from this little farm. He followed a six-year rotation: First year, fallow; second year, wheat; third year, barley; fourth year, oats which were sown to grass; fifth and sixth years, pasturage and hay. This rotation is not so well arranged as it might be. As is the case on all other successful small farms, nothing is allowed to go to waste. Every particle of manure is saved and applied to the land. The solid manure is for the most part put on the fallow ground, as this is to be sown in wheat. The liquid manure is applied to the pasture in the spring.

FARM OF RASMUS ANDERSEN.

Rasmus Andersen, in the hamlet of Tressebólle, is one of the fore most farmers in that region, who also gives much attention to dairying. His farm is not so heavily stocked as is the case on some others. He owns 107 acres and this he works with five large horses, and he keeps from 20 to 25 milch cows, besides young stock and swine. He sells the milk to a neighboring coöperative dairy, except what is used in the household. During 1892 he sold milk for 4,489 crowns ($1,230) from 21 cows, being an average income of $58.50 per cow.

The cattle were of the red Danish breed and were superior animals. During the winter they were cared for as follows: At 6 a. m. they got a feed of wheat straw, and the milking took place while they ate this. About 7 o'clock they were watered, and immediately afterward they had a feed of chaffed barley or oat straw, which was moistened and mixed with the grain feed. The grain consisted of one-half pound of rape-seed cake, one-half pound of sunflower cake, 1 pound of bran, and 2 pounds of mixed barley and oats ground together. This was the ordinary grain feed which they had twice a day, but extra heavy milkers received a little more. When this was eaten they had a feed of hay, all they would eat up clean, and this was followed by a feed of straw, which completed the feeding for the forenoon. In the afternoon the same routine was repeated of straw, water, grain feed, or chaff, hay and straw, the milking taking place at 6 p. m. The cattle remained in the barn all winter, not being let out once. They were watered in the manger, which was built of tiling and water-tight. In the summer the cattle were lariated in the pasture and received no grain except when the pastures were short; but pains were taken to provide first-class clover pasture.

Mr. Andersen followed an eight-year rotation: First year, bare fallow, which was heavily manured and which received four plowings during the summer and was sown in wheat in the fall. I was struck with the heavy seeding which he practiced; he never sowed less than two bushels of wheat per acre and preferred broad casting to drilling;

second year, wheat; third year, barley, which was sown with clover and mixed grasses. In the fourth year this was pastured, and in the fifth year cut for hay and was then manured and plowed up in the fall; and the sixth year sown in soiling crops, consisting of oats and peas mixed, or oats and vetches. This was fed in the stable when the pastures were short. The ground was plowed as fast as cleared; and the seventh year it was sown in barley and a portion in carrots, which was followed the eighth year by oats.

Mr. Andersen was highly impressed with the value of carrots for both cattle and horses, and he was planting increasing areas in this crop and intended, as soon as practicable, to raise enough to give the cattle at least one feed daily all winter. He recommended especially a yellow variety called "Long Green Head." The cattle eat the tops, as well as the roots. He raised them in rows one and one-half feet apart.

FARM OF ANDERSEN BROS.

I next visited a farm near the village of Leibólle, owned by two brothers named Andersen, who worked it in company. Their farm consisted of 66 acres of land on which they kept three good horses, or sometimes four, sixteen cows, some six or eight head of young stock, besides some swine and a few sheep. Their cows were of the red Danish breed and were considered superior animals, several of them milking between 40 and 50 pounds each per day. Their milk was sold to a neighboring coöperative dairy at fixed prices. The receipts from these sixteen cows during the year 1891 were as follows, by months. I am able to give this as they kindly permitted me to look into their account books:

January, 265.96 crowns; February, 310.91 crowns; March, 398.84 crowns; April, 380.88 crowns; May, 346.38 crowns; June, 292.15 crowns; July, 273.64 crowns; August, 250.44 crowns; September, 239.00 crowns; October, 169.93 crowns; November, 226.99 crowns; December, 328.06 crowns; total, 3,483.20 crowns; to which should be added 864.88 crowns, as their pro rata share in the profits of the creamery for the year. Grand total, 4,348.08 crowns ($1,191) as the receipts from sixteen cows in one year. The cows were fed as follows: At 6 a. m. a feed of straw, which they ate while the milking proceeded. Next a feed of moistened chaff made from barley or oat straw mixed with the grain feed. The grain feed consisted of 2 pounds of sunflower cake and 2 pounds of bran. When this was eaten they were watered and after their water they had a feed of hay. In the afternoon about 3 o'clock each cow got a feed of 50 pounds of roots, mangels, or carrots, while they lasted; at 4 p. m., again moistened chaff and grain. This time the grain consisted of 1 pound of rape-seed cake and 3 pounds of equal parts of barley and oats ground together, then they were watered. Next followed a feed of hay, and lastly, about 6 p. m., a feed of straw. The cattle stand in the stable all winter. In summer they were tethered on good pasture until harvest, except for a period during the last of June and beginning of July, when they were again stabled and fed on soiling crops. After harvest they run loose in the stubble fields. They get 3 pounds of bran per head daily during the summer. All the manure produced upon the place was saved with great care. The urine from all the stock was collected in cisterns and applied to the grass lands in the spring. Their system of rotation was as follows: First year, fallow, which was plowed several times and manured, and in the fall sown to wheat. They seeded also very heavily, using seed wheat at the rate of 2½ bushels per acre. The yield of wheat one year with another had for several years averaged 55 bushels to the acre. Second year, wheat; third year, barley, which was sown at the same rate and yielded about 50 bushels to the acre; fourth year, mangels and potatoes and a soiling crop consisting of oats and vetches grown together, the three occupying nearly equal areas; fifth year, oats, which were sown at the rate of 4 bushels to the acre and yielded, on an average, upwards of 80 bushels to the acre. The oats were sown with grass and clover. Sixth year, grass, used for pasture and hay; and seventh, grass, used for pasture and hay, which ended the rotation, the pasture being broken in the fall of the seventh year and followed by fallow. The two young men who owned and worked this farm had received more than an average education and were fine types of the best class of small farmers.

FARM OF P. NIELSEN.

On leaving the island I met a prominent breeder at an inn and had an interesting talk with him in regard to his business; but I did not see his place or any of his stock, it being too much out of my way to go there. His name was P. Nielsen, and he lived in the village of Torpe, Langeland. He informed me that he owned 69 acres of land, on which he kept 14 cows and about 6 head of young stock, the number he usually reared annually. His cows were of the red Danish breed, and several of the best ones gave each between 10,000 and 11,000 pounds of milk per year. All of his stock were recorded in the herd-book and he sold his heifers at high prices. He managed his cows somewhat differently from what is customary there, in that he fed them oftener. Each cow in full milk got 6 pounds of mixed barley and oats ground together, 2 pounds of bran, and 2 pounds of sunflower cake daily, this being divided into three feeds. The first feed was given at 5 a. m., consisting of straw; next they had one-third of the grain mentioned, then three-fourths of a bushel of roots, then a small feed of hay and again a feed of straw, and this course was repeated twice more during the day. Mr. Nielsen followed a seven-year rotation: First year, fallow, which was manured and sown to wheat in the fall; second year, wheat; third year, oats, laid out with clover and grass; fourth year, pasture; fifth year, hay; sixth year, half roots and half barley and oats mixed, which is grown for feed; seventh year, barley. He stated that his yields were about as follows: Wheat, 50 bushels to the acre; oats, 70 to 75 bushels; barley, about 50 bushels. Mr. Nielsen was superintendent of one of the many "bull associations" which are common in the country and of which I have already written. His association was a stock company of farmers, who bought bulls of superior quality, to be used on the cattle in their herds. These bulls were boarded out at various places, always, however, with some member of the company. Mr. Nielsen's association owned seven such bulls. The service fee to members was 2 crowns, or about 55 cents, and to non-members it was about $1.35.

ESKELUND DAIRY FARM.

This farm, on the island of Funen, was cultivated by a tenant farmer, who was absent at the time of my visit, and the following facts in regard to the place were obtained from the foreman: The farm is 240 acres in extent, soil of only fair average quality. They kept 12 work horses, 3 brood mares, 50 head of dairy cows, 2 stock bulls, a varying number of young cattle, which, however, amounted to as many during the year as there were cows. The cattle were all highly-bred, herdbook stock, and all the calves were saved. Besides this they had from 50 to 60 head of swine and the usual complement of poultry of all kinds. This herd is known all over the country, it being one of the most highly-improved herds of the red Danish cattle. It has been bred with care for about fifty years, and the herd has acquired a uniformity in color and build which is not always found in highly-bred stock. All the cattle were solid red and of an average weight of between 1,000 and 1,100 pounds. They were stabled in a fine brick barn, where they remained all winter, not being let out for water. Their feed during the winter season was as follows: at 4 a. m. they got a feed of barley straw, which they ate while the milking was in progress. At 6:30 they were watered, after which they got a feed of grain, consisting of 2 pounds of barley and oats mixed and ground, 1 pound of bran, one-half pound of palm-nut cake, one-half pound of rape cake, and one-half pound of sunflower cake. After this came a feed of roots. At 8 a. m. a small feed of hay was given and at 8:30 a. m. straw. At 11:30 a. m. they were again watered. The afternoon feeding began at 1:30 p. m. with a feed of straw and then the rest in the order as given above, with the exception of water. The management of the calves is of interest. Up to 2 weeks old they were fed on milk from their dams, each calf getting his own mother's milk, but about the tenth day they begin to mix in skim milk, the quantity being daily increased until in a few days the sweet milk is entirely supplanted, when they continue to get warm skim milk three times daily. But no one calf is ever allowed more than 24 pounds in a day, and that much only when about 2 months old. Soon after the skim-milk feeding begins a little linseed-oil meal is mixed with it and later ground oats, with hay and roots constantly before them. When between 5 and 6 months old the skim milk is gradually replaced with whey, which they get for a few weeks. The calves are pastured in summer and receive, in addition, some oil meal and ground barley and oats mixed. The heifers are bred to calve at 2 years old, and they calve at all seasons in order to have a moderately regular supply of milk. It is no small amount of work to feed some 30 or 40 head of calves in the above manner, each one having his own special "bill of fare." I was told that all the young stock sold readily at high prices. Bulls often brought 700 crowns ($190) apiece. The tenant farmer, Mr. R. Christiansen, is one of the most enlightened men in the neighborhood. He exhibited his cattle at all the leading shows and always carried off prizes. In 1878 he was awarded a silver medal at the Paris Exposition for a herd he had sent there. The cropping of the farm was an eight-year rotation, beginning the first year with fallow, which was manured. It was followed the second year with wheat and rye, and the third year, barley. The fourth year it was again manured for soiling crops, consisting of oats and vetches mixed, or oats and peas and mangels; fifth year, mixed grain, barley and oats used for feed, and with this laid out to clover and grass; sixth year, hay; seventh, pasture, the cattle being tethered in the field; and eighth year, oats, which completed the rotation.

RAVNDROP VÆNZGE FARM.

In the same neighborhood I visited another farm owned by Mr. P. Nielsen. This farm consisted of 84 acres of only medium quality soil, it being rather light, but it sustained 4 good horses, 40 head of cattle of all ages, and a small herd of swine. The cattle were all of the red Danish breed, purely bred and recorded stock, and the herd contained some of the best individuals of that breed. It was in many respects a model place. The barn was fireproof, built of brick with iron posts and well lighted and ventilated, and the floor was made of cement, perfect drainage being provided. At the time of my visit he had 20 cows, 7 yearling heifers, 3 bulls, and 12 calves. Mr. Nielsen practiced in-and-in breeding closely and so far with the best results. The cattle were of the usual size of that breed, between 1,000 and 1,100 pounds avoirdupois in weight. They were fed as follows: The first feed was given at 7 a. m., which was a grain feed and consisted of one-half pound of rape-seed cake, one-half pound of palm-nut cake, 1 pound of sunflower cake, one-half pound of hemp-seed cake, three-fourths of a pound of cotton-seed cake, one-half pound of bran, and 1 pound of ground barley and oats. This was for the best cows, however, those not in full milk not getting so much. When this was eaten they had a feed of straw; third, about 25 pounds of mangels per head; fourth, a small feed of hay; fifth, water, and sixth, a feed of straw, which finished the feeding for the forenoon. At 3 p. m. the afternoon feeding began exactly in the same order as above, the last feed being straw, which was given at 5 p. m. They are watered in the stable, which is customary everywhere, and are not turned out all winter. They are milked three times a day both winter and summer. The first milking begins at 6 a. m. in the winter and at 4 a. m. in the summer. During the summer the cows which are in milk are let out two hours each day on good pasture; but for the rest of the time they are in barns where they are fed equal parts of palm-nut cake, sunflower cake, and bran to the amount of 4 or 5 pounds a day in two feeds. Besides this they get green clover, or green oats and vetches grown together, and some little hay. All the grain is fed dry. Heifers and cows not in milk are tethered in the pasture most of the time. In the beginning of the '60's Mr. Nielsen's father procured a couple of fine heifers, which became the foundation of this very interesting herd, and during the last fifteen years the herd has been bred in-and-in closely.

A few figures in regard to the feed and produce of this herd may be of interest.

Average consumption of feed and yield of milk per cow, including heifers and barren cows.

Year.	Grain and oil cake.	Roots.	Hay.	Green fodder.	Yield of milk.
	Pounds.	Pounds.	Pounds.	Pounds.	Pounds.
1883	3,033	4,620			7,870
1884	2,910	3,938			7,694
1885	2,904	4,103	607	12,914	7,887
1886	2,910	5,170	968	11,704	8,083
1887	2,922	11,110	484	12,056	8,082
1888	3,148	11,770	404	11,528	8,516
1889	2,447	10,560	610	17,875	8,373
1890	3,195	10,569	830	12,205	9,253
1891	2,663	9,534	1,479	11,616	8,322
1892	2,787	12,079	1,513	12,848	8,795

Yields of some of the individual cows in the herd.—"Tolly" gave as a two-year old, 8,195 pounds of milk avoirdupois; at 3 years, 9,473 pounds; at 4 years, 9,744 pounds; at 5 years, 11,327 pounds; at 6 years, 10,080 pounds; at 7 years, 11,982 pounds; at 8 years, 13,043 pounds; at 9 years, 13,171 pounds. The latter figure is her yield in 1892. "Habele" gave, as six-year old, in 1892, 12,056 pounds of milk. "Anmaette" at 9 years old in 1892, 12,219 pounds. "Purtse" at 8 years old in 1892, 11,044 pounds. These are some of the very best yields of the breed.

Mr. Nielsen practiced a six year rotation, as follows: First year, rye; second year, barley, for which he uses a light dressing of Chile saltpeter; third year, mangels; fourth year, oats, which is laid out with clover and grass; fifth year, hay; and sixth year, pasture until July, when it is manured and broken for rye, being plowed three times before seeding in the latter part of September. All the manure produced upon the place is carefully saved.

HOLEV FARM.

In the village of Holev, some miles from the city of Odense, is a farm belonging to Jens Hansen's widow, which is one of the many interesting smaller farms in the neighborhood. It is superintended by her son, a young man who has the advantage of a good education, but the credit for the present condition belongs to the young man's father, who died only two years ago. The farm contains 125 acres, 19 of which are taken up by building sites, garden, orchard, farmyard, and a large wood lot. The remaining 106 acres are under culture. On this they had, at the time of my visit, 7 work horses, 2 colts, 26 cows, 8 heifers, 6 bulls, and 12 calves, besides 19 head of hogs, several of which were brood sows. The cattle were all of the red Danish breed and recorded in the herdbook. Jens Hansen had been a noted breeder ever since 1838, but the present herd has been bred since 1852, when he purchased a cow which proved to be of superior value and from which most of the herd has sprung, though some ten years later he procured three other excellent cows, whose progeny are in the herd. The young stock sells at good prices. A choice heifer, or bull, frequently brings as much as $270. I saw a three-year-old bull there for which I was told they had been offered about $378, but refused the offer. The cattle are fed in the following manner: The first feed consists of straw and is given at 5 a. m. when they are milked, and afterwards the stable is cleaned. Next, they are watered at 7:30 a. m. and immediately after they get a grain feed consisting of one-half pound of rape-seed cake, one-half pound of palm-nut cake, one-half pound of sunflower cake, one-half pound of cocoanut cake, 1½ pounds of mixed barley and oats ground, and 1 pound of bran. At 8:30 a. m. they get a small feed of hay. At 9 they get about 25 pounds of mangels and at 10 a feed of straw. The stable is then closed and kept as quiet as possible until 12, when they are again milked. After another season of rest the feeding begins again at 2:30 p. m. and consists of the same material in the same order, with the exception that they get no hay, but instead a feed of straw. In the evening they are milked at 7:30.

In summer the herd is let out some time during the first half of May, but is taken in at night, if the season is cold and rainy. They are tethered on the pasture until after harvest, when they are turned loose in the stubble field. During hot weather and when the flies are bad they are taken in during the day and let out at night, and in the fall again they are taken in at night and are out only in the daytime. If the grass gives out in the latter part of June, as is often the case, then they are put in the stable and fed on soiling crops until the pastures improve. During the entire summer each cow gets from 4 to 6 pounds of grain daily, half of which is oil cake and the other half barley and oats mixed. As in former cases, already mentioned, the calves receive special care. Each calf is kept in a pen by itself and fed on its mother's milk until 2 weeks old. The whole milk is then gradually supplanted by skim milk, and in the course of eight to ten days they get nothing but skim milk. The quantity allowed them is also carefully graded. The first day they get but 1½ pounds of milk in three feeds. When a week old a thrifty calf is allowed 1½ pounds three times a day, and when 2 weeks old 4 pounds each time, three times daily. In addition to this, they get crushed oats and linseed cake, the latter stirred in the milk as soon as they will eat it, and a little cut roots and hay constantly kept before them. When a month old they get 8 pounds of skim milk at each feed, three times daily, the milk being warmed to the temperature of the body. They never get more milk than this at any age, but the grain is gradually increased to 2 pounds daily, besides what roots and hay they will eat. They get no water at all while they are fed milk. Fall calves, which have gone through this course of treatment during the winter, are put on pasture the following summer, but spring calves are kept in the barn all summer, and in addition to the above treatment get a little cut grass daily. The grain continues, however, all summer for those on pasture. The following winter the yearlings get 3 pounds grain daily each, and about 30 pounds of roots. The heifers are bred when 15 months old, and after they calve the grain is increased gradually, as they can take it, up to the normal feed for cows. The cows have a disposition to milk perpetually, but they are dried up for six weeks, during which time each gets 6 pounds grain daily and 40 pounds roots, if her dry season happens to be in the winter. Their service bulls were fed from 4 to 6 pounds of oats daily, but no oil cake or any other kind of grain; in addition to this they got 25 pounds of mangels and all the hay and straw they would eat.

The milk was creamed and churned at home. There was a convenient ice dairy in the basement of the dwelling house where the milk was set in the usual tall tin cans and skimmed by hand. There was no separator on the place. The following are the outputs of milk and butter for each month during the year 1892, in pounds avoirdupois. The milk yield does not include the sweet milk fed to the calves, nor the new milk from fresh cows:

Month.	Milk yield.	Used in household.	Milk creamed and churned.	Butter made.
	Pounds.	Pounds.	Pounds.	Pounds.
January	14,510	440	14,070	507
February	14,617	440	14,177	528
March	18,018	440	17,578	698
April	20,904	440	20,464	782
May	19,644	440	19,204	737
June	19,504	440	19,064	667
July	17,360	440	16,922	602
August	13,129	440	12,689	471
September	10,511	440	10,071	387
October	11,089	440	10,649	427
November	12,042	440	11,602	448
December	10,945	440	10,505	389

I was kindly permitted to draw these figures from their account book. The processes followed in the butter-making were the same as those already repeatedly described. The butter sold for the same prices as were realized by the large dairies. Cheese was made of the skim milk, but only for home use, though a small surplus had been sold during the year to the value of about $54.

The ground was cultivated in a seven-year rotation. First year, oats, for which the pasture had been broken the previous fall; second year, roots, chiefly mangels, but also some carrots and turnips, the first two being for the milch cows and the last for the young stock. This crop is manured; third, two-thirds of the field in barley and one-third sown in Italian rye grass and yellow clover; fourth, the two-thirds which was in barley was manured and sown with soiling crops, vetches, and oats mixed; fifth year, the one-third which was in grass during the third and fourth years of the rotation is broken and sown in barley, which is cut for hay in June, and the two-thirds which was in soiling crops lies fallow and is plowed two or three times, and the whole field sown in wheat or rye in the middle of September. Sixth, this rye field is fed off and half of it sown in red clover and grass and the remaining half sown with barley and oats mixed, which is laid out with grass; seventh year, all is in grass.

The milk yield, not of the best cows, but of the whole herd including heifers, barren cows, and those that aborted, has averaged the following amounts per head for the years mentioned, in pounds avoirdupois: In 1886, 7,453; in 1887, 8,525; in 1888, 8,074; in 1889, 6,921; in 1890, 7,067; in 1891, 7,619; in 1892, 8,145. This, of course, gives no indication of the yield of the best cows, which runs up to 10,000 and 11,000 pounds each.

To show the possibilities of such a dairy on a 100-acre farm I drew from their books the sales and prices realized during 1892:

Products sold.	Prices.
	Crowns.
7 young bulls	3,150
4 old cows	740
5 heifer calves	1,065
9 other calves	410
17 fat swine	1,339
5,738 pounds butter	5,049
Milk	24
Cheese	200
Total	11,977 ($3,282)

Cost of bran, grain, oil cake and all the feed bought for the herd 3,027 crowns ($829). The rest of the feed was produced upon the place. The herd is exhibited in all the leading shows in Denmark and sometimes in foreign countries. In 1879 representatives from this herd took first premium in London, England. Since 1859 the herd has twice taken sweepstakes, in competition with the whole country, and taken sixty-six other prizes, of which thirty-eight were first prizes.

HERMANS MINDE FARM.

This property is owned by a Mr. Hermansen, and is situated on the peninsula of Jutland, a few miles from the city of Fredericia. It is a beautiful place, with a large, rather imposing brick dwelling house, substantial brick barn, and supplied with all modern conveniences. The cow stable was especially large and airy, built of iron and brick, so as to be entirely fireproof, with a good floor, and well drained. The property consisted of 150 acres, which was worked with 6 horses, and there were at the time of my visit 36 head of dairy cows, 13 head of young stock, a few sheep, and some 30 swine. The cattle were treated in the following way: They were watered the first thing in the morning, at 5 a. m; then they were given a feed of grain consisting of one-half pound of rape-seed cake, 2 pounds of mixed barley and oats, ground, and 2 pounds of bran per head; after this they got a feed of straw, then a small feed of hay, then a feed of straw again, when they rested until 1 p. m. At this time they were again watered and then given the same routine of feeds as in the forenoon. Some roots were raised, but seldom enough to last through the winter. No beeves were fattened except such cows as did not prove profitable for the dairy. The herd remained in the stable all winter, and they were also stabled every night during the summer, when they were fed soiling crops and hay, the object being to save the manure. The cattle were of a rather mixed character, none of them pure bred, though most of them belonged to the red dairy breed. The average milk yield per cow approached 6,000 pounds avoirdupois. The dairy department was in charge of a grown daughter, who kindly gave me details concerning her management.

The dairy room was located in the basement, at one end of the dwelling house, and was very conveniently arranged. It was an ice dairy, a capacious ice house near by being filled every year. Instead of the cement basins to hold the ice water, large tubs were used. These have some advantages over the brick and cement basins. They are very much cheaper, in the first place, and they are more readily cleaned and can be moved to the most convenient point in the dairy. These tubs were a few inches taller than the milk cans and each would hold nine or ten cans (see Fig. 4). A deep, cool well supplied all the water wanted, of the purest kind. It was raised to a tank on top of the house by means of a pump worked by horse power and from this tank pipes supplied water wherever needed. At the time of my visit 28 cows were giving milk, but many of them were nearly dry. This number supplied 500 pounds of milk daily. As soon as it was received from the barn, and was strained and weighed, it was transferred to the cans, which were sunk in the ice basins, where it remained thirty-six hours; but the milk was skimmed three times during that time, at the expiration of twelve hours, twenty-four hours, and thirty-six hours. The cream was kept in ice water until enough was collected for a churning; then it was warmed to a temperature of 70° to 74° F., when half a gallon of buttermilk from last churning was added. It then stood for twenty-four hours packed in a hay mattress, the object being to keep it as nearly as possible at about 60° F. The process of souring was watched in the meantime and if too rapid the temperature was reduced. She churned, at that time of year, at 54° F. The churn was of the pattern already described; in fact, I saw no other styles anywhere. She churned by horse power, and the butter always came in about thirty minutes. The butter was removed from the buttermilk with a sieve and worked by hand. It received three workings. At the first one, the buttermilk was pressed out. Soon after this 4 per cent of salt was added and worked in a little. It was then put in a cooling box and about an hour later it received a final working, when it was packed in butter barrels of the customary form. It required about 27 pounds of milk to make a pound of butter. In the fall, when many of the cows were about to go dry, the milk was more difficult to manipulate; the cream did not rise so readily, nor did it churn so well. She then set the milk in shallow iron pans, of the style already described, the pans being used also for the reason that they save ice. The ice supply usually runs short at that time of the year. She had not found it necessary to use pure cream cultures. The butter was first class and usually brought about $1.08 per 100 pounds over the top quotation of butter by the exchange in Copenhagen.

All the skim milk which was not used in the household, or for pigs and calves, was made into cheese. Her process was as follows: The cheese vat was a round tub which could hold about 400 pounds. The milk was warmed to 86° F., when she added 12 per cent of buttermilk. Then she added four one-hundredths of a pound of rennet extract to 350 pounds of milk. It was then allowed to stand thirty minutes to coagulate, when the curd was stripped and the whole mass stirred for fifteen to twenty minutes until the whey became clear and the small grains of curd would break when pressed. The whey was then drawn off and the curd put at once in the cheese cup. Her practice differed at this point from most other cheese-makers in that she did not permit the curd to be worked before it was put under the press. This, she maintained, would make the cheese tough; nor should it be allowed to cool before it was put under the press. The pressure applied is very light at first, and in half an hour the cheese is taken out and turned and again placed in the press, this being repeated four times during the first day. The following morning it is taken out and weighed and put in strong brine, where it remains for two days. It is next placed on the shelves in the cheese room, where it is turned and wiped with a dry cloth every other day. She got 23 öre per Danish pound, for her skim-milk cheese, which is about equal to 6 cents per pound avoirdupois.

An eight-year rotation was followed on this farm. First year, oats, the ground being broken from grass the previous fall. The oats were sown very thick, at the rate of nearly 6 bushels to the acre, and the yield reached nearly 100 bushels per acre; second year, fallow and manured with some 14 to 16 tons of stable manure per acre in May or June, and the fallow was plowed five times during the summer; third year, wheat or rye, sown on the fallow the previous fall. About 3 bushels of seed wheat per acre were used and the usual yield was from 40 to 45 bushels per acre; fourth year, barley, the barley ground being manured after harvest before the fall plowing; fifth year, barley and oats mixed, this being grown for feed, and the land was laid out with clover and grass; sixth, pasture or hay; seventh year, pasture or hay; and eighth year, pasture or hay, the grassland being broken and manured late in the summer of the eighth year. The help on the farm consisted, first, of a herdsman, who tended the stock and did odd chores about the place; second, two men and a boy of some 17 years. These were kept the year round and got their board and lodging and the customary wages (about $60 a year). In the house were kept three hired girls. The butter consumed in the household averaged 660 pounds avoirdupois annually, and about 6,000 pounds was yearly sold for export at an average price of nearly 27 cents a pound. Fat swine were sold to the value of about $540 annually, besides what was made into bacon for home consumption. The sale of skim-milk cheese amounted to about $162 yearly, and what grain was sold would balance the feed bought.

DALUM AGRICULTURAL SCHOOL.

In conclusion I will add a few notes from the farm of Dalum Agricultural School, situated near the city of Odense. This is a private school owned by J. Peterson, who was president and head teacher. The foundation of it is a small farm of 80 acres, in connection with which the proprietor has erected buildings and engaged teachers for the instruction, in agriculture, of about 100 pupils. I shall speak more fully of the school under another heading, and will at present note only what I learned concerning their farm practice. Owing to the absence of the proprietor, who is himself also professor of agriculture, and takes charge of the management of the farm, I could not obtain as detailed an account of the place as I desired. As stated, the farm consisted of 80 acres, on which were kept, at the time of my visit, 26 cows, 1 bull, and 3 heifers, all of the red Danish dairy breed, and superior individuals. These cattle were treated as follows: They were milked at 5 a. m.; at 7 a. m. they got a grain feed consisting of three-quarters of a pound of rape-seed cake, 1 pound of sunflower seed cake, three-quarters of a pound of cotton-seed cake, 1 pound of hemp-seed cake, and 1½ pounds of bran, and immediately after 25 pounds of sliced mangels. When this was eaten they were watered and they then got

4 pounds of hay, which completed the feeding for the forenoon. They were again milked at 12, and about 3 o'clock the above feeding was repeated, with the exception that they received straw instead of hay. They were milked the third time at 8 p. m. The average annual yield per cow, of all ages, reached 7,700 pounds avoirdupois. After the milk had been strained and weighed in the dairy the noon and evening milkings were put in ice water until the following morning, when it, together with the morning's milk, was run through a small separator, the milk being first warmed to 90° F. The cream was at once cooled off and kept in ice water until the ferment was added. They used the pure ferment produced by Mr. Quist, of Skanderborg. When enough for churning had been gathered, it was warmed to 66° F., and the ferment was added. At the time of my visit the churning temperature was 57° F. The dairy is not considered part of the school, except during three months of the summer, when there is a special dairy class in attendance. The rotation followed on the farm was as follows: First year, barley, which was laid out with clover and grass; second year, part of this was pastured and part was cut for hay, the cattle being tethered on the pasture; third year, oats; fourth year part of it was in soiling crops, which consisted of mixed barley and oats, oats and vetches, and oats and peas, and part was sown in buckwheat and yellow mustard, which were used as pasture. These were sown at different times, and what remained after pasturing was plowed under for green manure. This is termed a "cultivated fallow," to which manure is applied in the fall; fifth year, wheat or rye; sixth year, barley; and seventh year, mangels and sugar beets, which they use for feed. All the manure from the stables is saved with the greatest care. Drains from cow stable, pig-pens and horse stables led to a large cistern where all the liquid was collected, and the solid manure was kept under a shed. The liquid was partly applied to the grass land and partly sprinkled on the solid manure. A portion of the farm, comprising some 5 acres, was in permanent meadow and to this the liquid manure had been liberally applied for a long time, and it was found that when thus applied it, after a time, lost its beneficial influence unless lime and phosphoric acid were also added.

COÖPERATIVE CREAMERIES.

I have so far confined myself to the description of private dairies, large and small. I shall now consider the organization and work of the large number of coöperative creameries throughout the country. It is chiefly these that benefit the small farmers. They are patronized by men who, as a rule, keep but a limited number of cows, say from one to fifteen or twenty head, though occasionally the milk from much larger farms is also worked up in these creameries. It is from this class of creameries that the bulk of the export butter comes, and it is really these that fix the standing of Danish butter in foreign countries. There are two classes of creameries, which are distinguished from each other only in ownership, but which are alike in methods of operation and all other characteristics, and they can therefore be treated together under the above heading. The first class is the coöperative creamery proper, which is owned in company by all those who deliver milk there. The second class is the kind so largely represented in America in which the creamery plant is owned by one man, or at most by a few individuals, who buy the milk from the farmers of the neighborhood. The former are called "Andels" creameries, which is, properly translated, coöperative creameries. The second class is called "Fælles" creameries, and the name denotes delivery of milk by several individuals to the same creamery. In the former class the producers of milk have a personal interest. Their profits depend upon the management of the institution. In the second class they have no direct interest—it is merely a place where they sell their milk at so much per hundredweight, and the owner takes all the financial responsibility. The latter class of creameries has constantly decreased in number, while the former class has constantly increased. When it was found that coöperative creameries could be conducted without disagreement among those interested, and on an economical basis which would yield the best attainable returns, everybody wanted to join them. The Fælles creamery was doomed to go. None were willing to grant profits to the creamery owner if they could just as well share them. The creamery owners, on the other hand, became obliged to pay so much for their milk, if they wanted any, that a profit was practically impossible, and it has not unfrequently happened that when the farmers did not get the prices they thought they ought to have, they have built a coöperative creamery to which they have sent their milk and left the other creamery owner out in the cold.

I have nowhere been able to obtain definite statistics in regard to the number of coöperative creameries in the country, but I have seen various estimates placing them at from 1,000 to 1,500, and I am inclined to believe that the latter figure is very nearly correct. The number of Fælles creameries, on the other hand, does not probably exceed 400.

All these structures are alike in their essential points, and one traveling in the country soon learns to recognize them afar off. There are the two-story brick buildings with short wings for engine-houses, and the imposing brick chimneys, which are invariably present. They are usually located near the highways, at some central point of the district contributing milk, and the arrangement of detail, which I shall describe more fully hereafter, is essentially the same in all of them. They differ, however, in capacity from about 300 cows up to 1,500 or even more. The Fælles creamery has been in operation there for many years, but it is only during the last ten years that the coöperative creameries have sprung into existence. The history of their beginning and later growth is exceedingly interesting.

ORIGIN AND GROWTH.

They had their origin in the desire on the part of the small farmer to make the most possible out of his dairy. He had the example of the larger farms before him, where the dairy had always been an important and well-paying branch. How would it be possible for him to get relatively as much out of his few cows as the large farmers got out of their cows? The latter found it economical to place the dairy in the hands of expert help who could make first-class butter, which would realize the top market price; but the wives of the small farmers were by no means expert dairywomen. Their butter could not compare in quality with that produced upon the larger farms, nor was there any hope of so improving their practice that any considerable number could be counted on to make first-class butter. The only way open was for the farmers in the district, who were all equally interested, to unite, build a creamery, and deliver their milk there for creaming and churning; and this was what they finally did. But it resulted in this through some intermediate steps. The first of these was taken during the winter of 1881–'82. A few farmers in a certain part of the peninsula, after consultation, conceived the idea of engaging an expert at a stated salary per year, who should go from farm to farm and give instruction in dairy methods, and act as joint adviser and agent for them all, which position was offered to a Mr. S. Andersen, an educated man in the neighborhood. He saw, however, the insuperable obstacles to this course. Even though each farmer might provide the necessary utensils and the proper accommodations for the dairy, still their wives and daughters, his prospective pupils, would not all be equally apt learners, and those who found that the enterprise did not bring the desired results would soon withdraw from the arrangement. So for a time it amounted to nothing. But Mr. Andersen made them the proposition that if they would furnish him with a proper creamery and allow him the necessary help he would receive and churn their milk under his personal supervision and for a stated yearly salary. After many meetings it was finally decided to adopt this plan. But it was found that a sufficient number of farmers to represent 400 cows could not be obtained, and Mr. Andersen refused to begin operations with a less number. Three hundred cows were subscribed at once, and there were one or two hundred more in the neighborhood, but their owners did not think well of this new and untried coöperative scheme. They were willing to sell their milk, but did not care to risk anything on the proposed plan. This obstacle was finally overcome by Mr. Andersen, who offered to buy their milk on his own account, and on this basis, partly "Fælles," the first coöperative creamery in Denmark was started in 1882.

It was a task of no little difficulty. There was no similar institution from which even a hint could be taken in regard to the best method of organization, or the drafting of the laws and regulations, which it became necessary to have ; but it was fortunate, very fortunate for the future of the enterprise, that those to whom this task or the first organization was assigned were able, far-seeing men. The constitution which was finally adopted proved to be so satisfactory that it has been more or less literally copied in the organization of all later coöperative creameries. This first plant, including building, machinery, and all dairy utensils, cost 8,000 crowns ($2,160). The enterprise proved to be a success from the start, and those farmers who at first hesitated to join the organization, but preferred to sell their milk, one after another joined the company, and by the end of the second year all who delivered milk there were members.

The coöperative creameries have benefited the Danish farmers in more ways than one. They have been educators in addition to being the means of augmenting their incomes. The common interest which they had in the creamery brought the farmers together in frequent consultation, at which the brighter and more enterprising minds among them influenced the easier-going ones to adopt better methods. It compelled those who had not been in the habit of keeping accounts to study the art of bookkeeping in order to assure themselves that they received pay for all the milk they delivered.

The constitution usually requires a minimum amount of oil cake to be fed daily to each cow, and this, of course, had to be bought. This raised the question of cost of feed and the return in milk from the feed given, questions which were to be closely studied. And now every Danish farmer interested in a coöperative creamery is able to tell to the fraction of a cent what his feed has cost him and what his returns in milk have been. Under the Fælles creamery system the farmers sold their milk directly to the creamery man. They were not particularly interested in the quality of the milk. No practical test had at that time been devised by which the amount of fat in the milk could be ascertained with ease and certainty. Under the coöperative system they soon recognized that the milk from some herds was worth more for butter than from others, and, since butter was the product aimed at, they all conceded the equity of paying for the milk in accordance with the per cent of fat it contained. At this juncture Prof. Fjord came to their assistance by inventing his "control" apparatus, which has already been described (Fig. 12) in the foregoing pages, and his invention is now in use in every creamery in the land. Indirectly this testing apparatus led to the improvement of the cattle. When one farmer found that his neighbor received more money for his milk than he, it was natural to inquire into the cause, which, in most cases, was traced to the cow herself. This, again, led to the organization of numerous societies for the improvement of the cattle, one form of which is represented by the "bull associations" already mentioned; and thus one question suggested another until the present standard has been reached. But they will by no means stop here. The same forces are still at work. Improvement in every line of the dairy interest is the ambition of the whole country. It is this wholesome development of the coöperative creameries which has increased the Danish exports of butter to the present astonishing figures, the amount having almost doubled during the last half-dozen years.

ORGANIZATION—OFFICERS, SALARIES, ETC.

When an organization is to be effected the farmers of the neighborhood meet together, and, having agreed upon the general plan, they elect a board of directors from their number. There is considerable difference, numerically, in the composition of this board in different organizations. Thus, the number of directors varies from three to fifteen. This board is charged with the duty of conducting the business of the creamery according to the requirements of the constitution which the organization adopts. A chairman, a secretary, and a treasurer are elected from among the board of directors. In some cases a small salary is paid to each, while in other cases they give their services. The board of directors hire a competent dairyman to take charge of the creamery. He, in all cases that came under my observation, had rooms in the building. Sometimes he is paid a salary only, at other times he is paid both salary and commission, this latter plan being the most common. He gets his commission from the surplus which the butter brings over the highest quotation on the exchange in Copenhagen, and he thus becomes financially interested in producing the finest quality possible. He also has certain allowances of milk and butter, and is furnished fuel, light, etc.

The salary of such a man will vary from $270 to $405 a year, in addition to his commission; or from $432 to $1,080 a year when he works without a commission. The board of directors hold him responsible for the operation of the creamery. According to the terms of the agreement he is either allowed a given sum with which to hire his helpers, or, as happens in many cases, he supplies the helpers himself and pays them out of his own pocket. In any case he is the only responsible person. When he pays for the help it is very generally the case that he gets young men and women who desire to learn the business and who work for a small salary in order to get the benefit of his instruction and become familiar with the details of the business.

The capital with which the plant is erected is, in nearly all cases, money borrowed at 4 per cent interest. The terms of the agreement usually require that a given amount shall be paid off each year for a period running from ten to twenty years, and each member of the organization becomes personally responsible for a share of the capital thus borrowed, in proportion to the number of cows that he has entered. In the meetings of the organization the members vote also by the number of cows represented by each, or, in some cases, by the square root of the number of cows represented by each. When new members wish to join a body already organized, they must obtain their places by paying a certain amount of cash into the treasury of the association. The value of the partnership is usually based upon the amount of milk delivered and the profits made during the year preceding.

The methods of procedure in these creameries are so nearly alike that only a few examples are necessary to convey an idea of them.

KILDEVÆLD COÖPERATIVE CREAMERY.

This is a typical creamery, on the island of Zealand, some 12 or 14 miles from the city of Hilleród. I investigated this institution thoroughly, and am under obligations both to the president of the board of directors, Mr. M. F. J. Grónbeck, and to the superintendent in charge of the creamery, Mr. L. H. Larsen, who, with unreserved kindness, answered all my questions fully.

The building was a two-story brick, much like the pattern shown in Figs. 24, 25, and 26 (pp. 109, 110), although these illustrations are not identical with the building in question. The lower floor was devoted to the dairy alone. It was level with the ground, and was divided into only two rooms, the larger one of which contained the separator and the churn, and there also the milk was received. In the smaller room the butter was worked, cooled, and stored until shipment. A small "L" projecting back from the main wing contained the boiler and engine with storage room for coal, and back of this was an ice house. The necessary water was supplied by a good well, from which it was pumped by the engine into a suitable reservoir. The upper story was set apart for the superintendent and his family and also contained rooms for the helpers.

President Grónbeck kindly furnished me with the following facts concerning the plant: The association was organized in 1888, with 69 members, representing 400 cows; but, as they anticipated that others would join, they decided to erect a creamery with a capacity for 1,000 cows.

At first it was agreed that each member should pay into the treasury a sum of 27 cents per cow owned by him. This was raised to 54 cents, and later to $1.35 per cow. The following is a statement of capital and expenses of the plant:

Capital.

Assessment of members at $1.35 per cow	$675.00
Loan from bank	8,640.00
Total	9,315.00

Expenses.

12,000 sq. ft. of ground for buildings and garden	$400.92
Cost of buildings	3,995.40
Cost of machinery	3,148.82
Furniture	434.09
Wagons, milk cans, and utensils	1,052.85
Miscellaneous	133.71
	9,165.79
Later improvements	1,080.00
Total	10,245.79

The later improvements have been made from the profits of the business. The buildings have been constructed in the most substantial manner, and the machinery is the best obtainable. The business is in the hands of a board of directors, who elect their own chairman, secretary, and treasurer, and their actions are binding on the association.

The creamery began business the first of November, 1888, with 69 members, representing 400 cows, and in February, 1893, there were 177 members, representing 1,400 cows. The superintendent of the creamery was hired by the board of directors, and he had direct charge of the work in the creamery. His salary consisted in 6 per cent of the value of the butter made from the "overskud" (surplus). This term "overskud," which may be translated "surplus," is, when used in this sense, a little difficult to understand. They estimate that it requires 28 pounds of milk to make a pound of butter. Now if the creamery superintendent can make a pound of butter from 25 or 26 pounds of milk, the difference between that and the estimated 28 pounds is called the "surplus," and his wages consisted of 6 per cent of this and 20 per cent of the price which his butter realized more than the highest quotation made by the exchange in Copenhagen each respective week; in addition, he had furnished quarters, fuel, light, milk, butter, garden, etc., but out of this he paid for his hired help. The members of the company were paid for their milk once in four weeks, according to the per cent of fat in the milk, calculated by the system invented by Prof. Fjord. They got the price of a pound of butter for every 28 pounds of milk of average per cent fat, the highest quotation of the exchange each week fixing the price of butter; and if there was still a surplus in the treasury it was divided among the members in the form of a dividend twice yearly. In this creamery there had so far always been a considerable dividend distributed in this manner. The members were bound to take back their proportion of the skim milk and the buttermilk, and for this they paid the creamery 1 öre per pound, a trifle more than one-fourth of a cent.

The creamery provided the cans, fetched the milk from each farm, and brought each man back his proportion of the skim milk and the buttermilk; but the teams used were hired and paid for at the rate of

19 öre per 100 pounds of milk hauled. The skim milk was sterilized before it was returned, by being heated to a temperature 190° F. as fast as it ran from the separator. These were the fundamental principles on which the creamery was run, all of which I learned from the president of the company.

CONSTITUTION OF KILDEVÆLD CREAMERY.

To give a still clearer idea of the workings of a coöperative creamery I insert the following translation of the constitution of Kildevæld Creamery:

First. The object of the association is to secure to its members the best possible returns from their dairy cows. The milk shall be separated in common and from the cream butter shall be made and marketed. The members shall take back their proportion of the skim milk and buttermilk and shall pay for the same at about their actual value.

Second. Any one can become a member of this association by paying 1 crown per cow which he proposes to enter; provided, however, that not fewer than two-thirds of the votes cast are in his favor. But all who join after the creamery begins business shall pay 5 crowns per cow into the association's treasury. Each member shall on all occasions be entitled to vote as follows:

	Votes.
From 1 to 10 cows	1
From 11 to 20 cows	2
From 21 to 40 cows	3
From 41 cows upwards	4

Third. The association shall elect from their number a board of directors consisting of five members, and this board shall elect its own chairman, secretary, and treasurer, which offices must not be united in the same person. The board of directors shall represent the association in all business affairs, and their action shall be binding on the association. No member shall refuse to hold office when duly elected. The board of directors shall hold office five years, and the term of one of the original board shall expire each year during the first term, as determined by lot. Those who have once held office may decline reëlection if they choose. The board of directors shall receive no pay, but they may employ a bookkeeper, at a salary not to exceed 40 öre per cow, and all necessary expenses incurred for the association shall be refunded from the treasury.

Fourth. An annual meeting of all the members shall be held each year in February, at which meeting the board of directors shall give an account of the business done during the past year and present plans for the business during the current year. At these meetings all differences that may arise between the board and members, or between the members themselves, shall be settled, and the meeting shall appoint an assessor and two auditors, the latter to hold office for two years, and one of those first appointed shall resign at the end of one year, as determined by lot. Amendments to the constitution shall require a two-thirds majority, but all other questions, not otherwise specified, are to be determined by a simple majority of the votes cast. Extraordinary meetings may be held at the call of the board, or upon the written request to the board of not less than one-third of the members. The board shall then give at least ten days' notice of the meeting to each member, who shall also be notified of the purposes of the meeting.

Fifth. The board shall contract a loan as large as necessary for the erection of the contemplated plant. For this loan each member shall be responsible, in proportion to the number of cows he enters, until all is paid.

Sixth. If a member sells or transfers his property, his share in the creamery shall pass to the new owner, if the latter will accept the privileges and responsibilities it confers; if not, the association shall pay the outgoing member only one-half of his share. No member can withdraw from the association before the debt is paid, except by removal from the neighborhood. Members desiring to withdraw after the debt is paid shall give at least three months' written notice of such withdrawal to the board of directors, and they shall be entitled to only one-half of their share from the association. Members who are expelled by the annual meeting shall lose their shares.

Seventh. The board of directors shall hire a superintendent for the creamery, who shall keep account with the members and shall be responsible for the work in the creamery. The superintendent shall hire, pay, and board all his help. He shall have at least one assistant who is a competent butter-maker, and at least one other assistant who is competent to take charge of the machinery (engineer). The superintendent of the creamery shall be paid quarterly, and shall be furnished quarters with garden, fuel and light, and the creamery products necessary for his household, and at the end of the year, when accounts are balanced, he shall be paid a premium for every hundred pounds butter sold at a satisfactory price.

Eighth. The milk shall be paid for in accordance with its content of fat, which shall be determined by the superintendent of the creamery. Milk of the average per cent of fat shall be paid for at the rate of the highest quotation for a pound of butter for each 28 pounds of milk.

Ninth. Until the debt of the creamery is paid the members shall be bound to receive their respective portions of skim milk and buttermilk, for which they shall pay about one-third of a cent per pound. After the debt is paid the price of this milk can be fixed at each annual meeting.

Tenth. The rates fixed in paragraphs 8 and 9 presuppose that there will be a surplus in the treasury over and above what is paid for the milk. This surplus shall be employed to cover current expenses, to pay interest, as well as the principal of the debt, as it falls due, or it may be divided among the members.

Eleventh. When the debt is paid, the president of the board, the assessor, and superintendent of the creamery shall assess the property of the company, which shall be assigned to the members in proportion to the amount of milk each has delivered since the business began. Thereafter the yearly profits shall be divided so that each member shall receive, first, 5 per cent of the value of his share, and if there is still a surplus in the treasury it shall be divided among the members in proportion to the amount of milk each has delivered during the past year.

Twelfth. The association shall provide and maintain the necessary number of milk cans and shall transport the milk to and from each farm; however, members who deliver less than 100 pounds of milk daily shall bring their milk to the nearest point on the highway where the transport wagons pass, and shall receive the skim milk in the same place. Members located off the main road shall keep the roads to their respective farms open and passable, and the milk cans shall be ready for the driver when he calls at the time named the day before.

Thirteenth. It shall be the duty of each member to keep his milk cans scrupulously clean, to see that strict cleanliness is observed in milking, and to strain the milk at once into the milk cans and place these in cold water, which shall be changed if necessary. Milk from sick cows must not be sent to the creamery, and milk from fresh cows must not be sent until four days after calving. It shall be the duty of the superintendent of the creamery to see that the milk is sweet and good. If the cans are not properly cleaned, or if the milk is objectionable, he shall give written notice thereof to the members interested, and if the fault is not corrected at once he shall refuse to receive the milk. If this happens a second time such member shall be fined two crowns for each cow in his herd. The members are forbidden to make butter or cheese for sale, and also to sell sweet milk to other creameries; but they are allowed to retain what they desire for use in the household and to give away milk to poor people who do not keep cows. If desired, the members have the right to get their butter from the creamery at the same price that it will then bring on the market.

Fourteenth. It shall be the duty of the members to feed their cows in such a manner that the milk shall not be affected disadvantageously or the quality of the butter deteriorated. Cabbage, turnip tops, and kohlrabi tops must not be fed. Members shall notify the superintendent of the creamery of changes in feed, and keep him informed concerning the feeds used, so that he may give special attention to the milk. If the feed affects the quality of the milk or the butter, it shall be the duty of the superintendent to give written notice thereof to the member in question, and if the fault continues he shall refuse to receive the milk. The president of the board and the superintendent may, when they agree, forbid the use of any feed which they have reason to think is detrimental to the creamery. Members who refuse to be governed by their decision, or who do not live up to the regulation of this paragraph, shall be fined from two to ten crowns per cow, and pay for the injury they have caused the creamery as estimated by the president of the board, the superintendent of the creamery, and the assessor.

Fifteenth. To enable the members to obtain good feed stuffs at the lowest rate, the board, or a committee appointed for the purpose, may purchase such feeds at wholesale for the benefit of the members. It shall further be the duty of the members to buy rape-seed cakes enough for each cow to have at least one pound daily all the year through, and it shall be the duty of the board of directors to aid the members in feeding their cattle in an intelligent and economical manner, and, for example, by the purchase of seed, aid in the culture and use of plants which have a desirable influence on the quality of the butter.

Sixteenth. It shall be the right and duty of the board of directors and the superintendent of the creamery to inspect the premises of each member as often as they see fit, to note the quality of their fodder, pastures, cleanliness in stables and milk room, etc., and each member shall give all the information they may desire on these subjects, and if it can be proved that a member has withheld information wanted, or given them wrong information in regard to these matters, he shall be fined from two to ten crowns per cow and pay for the injury he may have caused the creamery, according to the estimates made by the president, superintendent, and the assessor.

Seventeenth. If any contagious disease appears either among the people or the cattle, on a member's farm, it shall be his duty to stop the delivery of milk at once until the disease has disappeared and proper disinfection taken place, and in case such disease appears at the creamery, the superintendent shall cause the sick person to be moved away and the place to be disinfected. To prevent possible transportation of disease in the milk, the skim milk shall be sterilized at the creamery before it is returned to the members. Non-compliance with the provisions of this paragraph shall be punished by fine in an amount not to exceed 100 crowns.

Eighteenth. It shall be the duty of the board to oversee the management of the superintendent and to see that the machinery and utensils are at all times in satisfactory condition, and particularly shall it be the duty of the board to give the whole creamery a thorough overhauling in regard to repairs every spring so that it may be in good condition for the warm season. At the close of the yearly account an inventory of the property owned by the association shall be taken jointly by the president of the board, the superintendent of the creamery, and the assessor, so that the members may always have a correct idea of the value of their common property.

Nineteenth. It shall be the duty of the board of directors to see that the cash on hand is employed to the best advantage of their association. The members shall be paid every four weeks for the amount of milk they have delivered, less the value of the products they have received from the creamery. Division of the profits shall take place yearly after the annual meeting of the association.

Twentieth. In all cases when points arise not covered by this constitution the board of directors shall use their best judgment in the interest of the association, and, if necessary, bring the matter up at the next annual meeting, which alone is empowered to make alterations in or additions to these regulations.

Twenty-first. The board of directors shall have authority to buy milk for the creamery from farmers who are not members of the association.

Twenty-second. This constitution shall go into effect on and after the 27th of May, 1888.

I would call especial attention to those paragraphs in this constitution which are intended to enforce cleanliness in the handling of the milk, and which aim to compel the farmer to feed his cattle in such a manner that the milk shall not be objectionable. It is worthy of note that the board of directors are empowered to impose fines severe enough to deter any slovenly or careless person from breaking the rules. The fact that none can withdraw from the association until the debt is paid, except by removal from the neighborhood, unless he is willing to lose half his vested interest in the concern, is a feature which could probably not be put in force in this country.

All the essential features in this constitution are found in the constitutions of all the coöperative creameries, and although this represents but one of the many hundreds of associations which there are in the country, it is, nevertheless, a type of them all.

PRACTICAL OPERATIONS OF KILDEVÆLD CREAMERY.

The superintendent of Kildevæld creamery, Mr. L. H. Larsen, kindly gave me the following details concerning the operations of the creamery:

Although there were 1,400 cows entered by the members of the association, the creamery was receiving milk from only about 1,300 of them at the time of my visit, and from this number they obtain in round numbers 18,000 pounds of milk daily. A large majority of the members had only from 1 to 10 cows. A few had from 20 to 30 cows, but there were only two larger farms which contributed to the creamery, on one of which there were 60 cows and on the other 80. It will thus be seen that it was especially the small farmer, with only a few acres of land, who profited by the coöperative system. At that time of the year (February) it required 27 pounds of milk to make a pound of butter. The milk from all these patrons was tested twice each week, but the patrons did not know from what deliveries the samples were taken. They were paid in proportion to the per cent of fat contained in the milk. For this analysis Fjord's control apparatus was used, by means of which 192 samples could be tested at once. (See Fig. 12.) This apparatus can be used only in connection with the Burmeister & Waine separator, this machine having a larger bowl than the others. The bowl is filled with water heated to a temperature of 133° F., the tubes of milk being warmed by it to this temperature. The separator is then run at a low speed, 1,500 revolutions per minute, for three-quarters of an hour. The cream has then formed a hard, perfectly solid mass in the opening of the tube. The thickness of this mass of cream is measured by means of a scale applied to the glass, and by reference to a table constructed by Prof. Fjord the per cent of fat can be told with accuracy.

All the patrons milk their cows three times a day, and the noon and the evening milk is kept in cold water, or ice water at the farms, until the following morning, when the transport wagon arrives and takes it, together with that morning's milk. As already stated, the creamery owns the cans and transport wagons, but the teams and drivers are hired and remunerated at from 5 to 7 cents per 100 pounds of milk hauled, according to the length of the route. All milk is tested upon its arrival at the creamery. If something is found wrong with it, and the superintendent is disposed to think that it is caused by one or more cows in the herd, he sends a case of small bottles to the farm and each cow's milk is sampled, and upon the return of these samples to the creamery the fault can frequently be traced to some individual animal, and her milk is then excluded until the fault is remedied. The milk furnished by each patron is of course weighed and the weight entered in the record.

From the receiving vat the milk runs through the "forewarmer," where it is heated to 84° F. in winter and 80° F. in summer before it runs through the separator. There were four of the Burmeister & Waine separators in use. From the separator the cream is discharged into tall cans which are sunk in ice water, one after another, as they are filled. The skim milk is raised by the separators themselves to a tank on the same level as the receiving platform, from which it runs through a pasteurizing apparatus, where it is heated to 190° F. From this it is discharged into a large tank from which the amount due each patron is weighed out and sent back. The price, as already mentioned, was one öre per Danish pound. There was no difficulty in getting the patrons to take the milk at this price and some were glad to get more than their share. This milk reaches the farms perfectly fresh and sweet. It is used largely for the manufacture of skim-milk cheese and to feed to calves and pigs. The buttermilk is in like manner returned to the patrons at the price given for skim milk.

When all the cream had been separated and cooled, about noon, the ferment was started. To this end the cream was first warmed to 64° F. In this creamery they used the somewhat troublesome method of warming it by setting the cans in hot water and constantly stirring their contents and testing with the thermometer until the desired temperature was reached. In most other places they used a pasteurizing apparatus for this purpose. When the proper temperature was reached the prepared ferment was added, to the amount of from 6 to 8 per cent of the weight of the cream, and it then stood in the cream barrels for 18 hours, from noon until 6 the following morning, when the churning began. Mr. Larsen used pure culture ferment for his cream. He propagated this ferment from day to day in skim milk, and he found it necessary to buy new cultures only once in about two months. For propagating this ferment he used 200 pounds of fresh milk daily. This was secured from special cows which had calved only four or five weeks. He used the morning's milk. It was set in cold water immediately on arrival and skimmed by hand. After skimming it was pasteurized at 176° F. and then kept in warm water of the same temperature for 15 minutes, after which it was cooled to 82° F., when a portion of the ferment made in the same manner the previous day was added. This ferment was added about 2 p. m. The skim milk containing the ferment was then warmed to 88° F. by setting the cans in warm water, and by means of a steam pipe connected with the water-tank it was kept at the temperature until evening, when it was thick. It was then taken out of the warm water and set in cold water of about 50° F., where it remained until the next noon, when it was ready to be added to the cream. He considered this the best method. He deprecated the use of buttermilk as a starter, and would never use it unless compelled to do so.

The churns are started at between 5 and 6 a. m. At that season he churned at a temperature of 57° F., but in summer he frequently went as low as 52° F. The churning temperature varied with the character of the butter and with the weather. He judged of the required temperature by the character of the butter. The creamery was furnished with four churns of the pattern already described. The dasher in each made 130 revolutions per minute, at which speed it required forty-five minutes to churn. When the butter began to form in small granules the size of pin heads, the churns were stopped and the sides and lids were washed down with water at a temperature of about 50° F. Each churn contained from 400 to 450 pounds of cream, which filled it about three-quarters full. The butter was dipped out of the churn with a sieve or strainer and immediately worked a little on the butter worker to remove most of the buttermilk. It was then weighed and four and a half per cent of salt added, which was worked in lightly. The butter was next made into crescent-shaped rolls and placed in ice boxes made for that purpose (see Fig. 16). Here it stood for two hours, after which it was worked for the last time and at once packed in barrels holding about 110 pounds each. The butter was sent off every Monday. It was sold to a dealer in Copenhagen, who paid about $1.00 per 100 pounds above the highest quotation on the exchange for the preceding week. The cream in this dairy was not pasteurized before it was churned. All unfavorable conditions were so well under control that this was not found necessary. The leading pieces of machinery and apparatus in this creamery were as follows:

(1) An 8-horse power engine.
(2) A 10-horse power boiler.
(3) Four "B. & W." separators, each with a capacity of 4,000 pounds per hour, when run at a speed of 2,700 revolutions per minute.
(4) Four churns of the usual pattern.
(5) One "forewarming" apparatus for sweet milk.
(6) Two Pasteurizing machines for the skim milk.
(7) Three large milk vats, one each for sweet milk, skim milk, and buttermilk, besides several smaller ones used as occasion demanded.
(8) Eight cream barrels.
(9) One large butter-worker.
(10) Several ice boxes in which to cool butter.
(11) Three large water-tanks for cold and warm water.
(12) Forty cream cans.
(13) Six hundred cans used in the transportation of milk. They varied in capacity from 40 to 100 pounds.

Besides these, there was a large reservoir on top of the building which was always kept full of water, pumped by steam from a good well, and with this tank there were connections to all parts of the creamery where cold water was needed. In like manner a hot-water tank furnished hot water to all parts of the creamery, and there was a miscellaneous collection of smaller utensils not necessary to specify.

The working force of the creamery consisted of, first, the superintendent; second, an engineer, who had charge not only of the engine and boiler but also of the separators; third, a weighmaster, who weighed all the milk that came in or left the creamery and assisted with other things; fourth, a butter-maker; fifth, an assistant who had no special duties; sixth, two pupils, a young woman and a young man, who worked, however, the full time as did the others. All of these people received their pay, board and lodging from the superintendent of the creamery. The pupils got their board and a very small wage besides, for which they worked as much as would be required of a hired person. The other four assistants were paid according to their value, the total amount paid to all being about $300 per year, besides board and lodging.

The accompanying summary of the business of the creamery for the years 1889, 1890 and 1891, which I obtained permission of Mr. Larsen to transcribe from his books, will give a clear idea of the profit to the patrons as well as the business of the creamery in a more condensed form than any description could give.

Information from Kildevæld creamery.

General statistics.	1888-'89.	1889-'90.	1890-'91.
Pounds sweet milk delivered	4,614,831	5,712,081	6,395,909
Average number pounds received daily	12,643	15,649	17,523
Average number pounds received from each member	134	173	179
Number of cows	945	1,115	1,240
Average number pounds from each cow per day	13.37	13.53	14.22
Number pounds per cow per year	4,883.40	4,939.50	5,157.90
Pounds milk required for each pound butter	29.31	30.12	29.39
Receipts per 1,000 pounds of milk.			
Butter	$9.93	$9.33	$9.91
Skim milk and buttermilk	2.57	2.57	2.60
Total	12.54	11.90	12.51
Expenses per 1,000 pounds of milk.			
Transportation	$0.29	$0.35	$0.37
Fuel	.18	.15	.15
Wages	.22	.20	.22
Butter packages	.18	.14	.16
Capital and interest due	.10	.17	.16
Repairs	.14	.21	.05
Total	1.11	1.22	1.11
Cost of making 1 pound butter	0.027	0.03	0.027
Paid to members	10.37	9.69	10.34

A TYPICAL COÖPERATIVE CREAMERY.

I append here illustrations of a coöperative creamery calculated to handle the milk from about 700 cows. I did not find time to visit this creamery, but the illustrations presented, with their explanations, will serve to convey an idea of the construction and equipment of the typi-

FIG. 24.—A typical coöperative creamery.

cal coöperative creamery. Fig. 24 gives a front view of the building. On the left is seen the driveway in which the milk is delivered. There are rooms above for the accommodation of the superintendent and help. Fig. 25 shows a section of the same building with some of the apparatus in place. Fig. 26 shows a ground plan of the same. *A* is a stable, *B* coal room, *C* driveway, *D* the main dairy room, *E* butter room, *F* cheese room with cellar below, *G* office, and *H* a raised platform on which

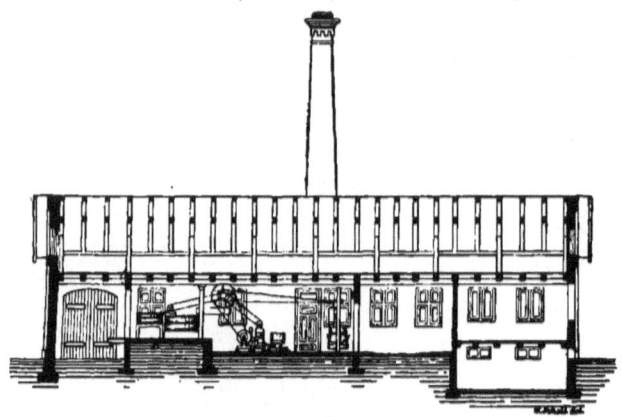

Fig. 25.—Section of typical coöperative creamery.

the milk is received and weighed. The machinery is designated as follows: a_1 and a_2 two separators, b a forewarmer, c_1 and c_2 represent two churns, d cheese vat, e vat for sweet milk, f vat for skim milk, g tank for hot water, h butter worker, and s sterilizing apparatus.

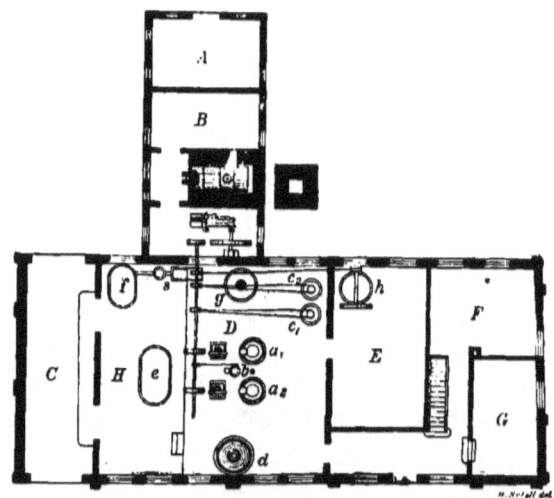

Fig. 26.—Ground plan of typical coöperative creamery.

I will here add an illustration (Fig. 27) which has been prepared by H. C. Petersen & Co., manufacturers of creamery goods, Copenhagen. It shows the arrangement of the machinery in a well-equipped dairy, and although it is an idealistic arrangement it corresponds with the arrangement generally found in the coöperative creameries. It is best studied by following the milk and cream through the various machines. The milk is carried from the delivery wagon A to the weigh box C, into which it is emptied. From this it runs into the vat for sweet milk D, and through the pipe d into the forewarmer E, and from this into the separator F. The skim milk rises of itself through the pipe L and through the trough l into a small suspended vat M. This vat is found necessary in order to give the froth time to settle. From this it runs into the pasteurizing apparatus N and from here over the cooler O into the skim milk vat P. From this it is drawn into the cans R and weighed on the scale S and then disposed of to customers. If cheese is made, the skim milk runs directly into the cheese vat from the sepa-

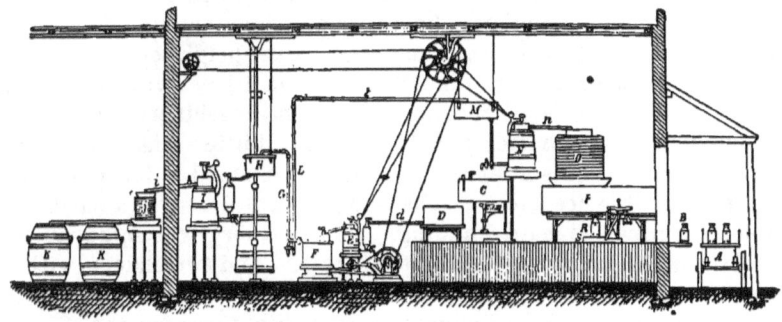

FIG. 27.—Arrangement of machinery in creamery.

rator. The cream leaves the separator through the pipe G into the small suspended vat H. From this it runs through the pasteurizing apparatus I over the cooler j and through the trough j into the cream barrels at K. The whole is arranged on the gravity plan, so that the milk or cream can run of itself to any place it may be wanted.

RENKOLDE COÖPERATIVE CREAMERY.

I mentioned this creamery briefly in my preliminary report. It is organized exactly on the plan just described and run on the same methods. The plant consisted of a large, substantial brick building with rooms for the superintendent and help. The ground and building with ice house cost about $5,400 and the machinery $2,835 and later additions and utensils and improvements cost $405, making a total of $8,640. All this money was borrowed from a bank at 4 per cent interest, to be paid off in sixteen years, at the rate of $540 per year. It had been running only a few years, but had so far been entirely successful. The patrons were paid the maximum quotation per pound of butter for 28 pounds of milk, 28 pounds being the standard assumed as necessary to make a pound of butter. It is, however, only in a few instances that it requires that much milk. The superintendent was paid a certain per cent of the profits, as is usually the case, and he hired his help, which consisted of two men and two women. During the past year the surplus, after paying the patrons at the rate stated above for milk delivered, was sufficient not only to pay all running expenses, but to pay the interest, the $540 falling due on the capital invested, and still give each patron a dividend of about 17 cents for each 100 pounds of milk delivered. The superintendent informed me that he, at that time of year, only used 25 pounds of milk to a pound of butter, and that in summer he used 29.5 pounds. They received, at that time, milk from about 1,100 cows daily, from which they made on an average 350 pounds of butter per day. The arrangement of the building was the same in pattern as the one already described, with only slight differences. Near the center of the building was an arched gateway for the wagons to drive through, and on one side of this was the creamery and on the other the rooms for the superintendent and his help. The delivery and weight platform was raised to the height of a wagon box, but the other portions of the building were on a level with the ground. There was first a large room, in which the machinery was placed. Beyond this was a butter room, where the butter was worked and packed. Next to this a storage room, which stood in immediate connection with the ice house. The engine was placed in a small "L" projecting from the main building. The creamery was equipped with an eight horse-power engine, three separators, and two churns, with the necessary smaller utensils, water tanks, etc. The skim milk and buttermilk were taken back by the patrons who paid three-fourths of an öre per pound.

RINGE COÖPERATIVE CREAMERY.

On the island of Funen I visited a representative coöperative dairy in the village of Ringe, where Superintendent L. Rasmussen kindly gave me the following details in regard to the business: The building was of brick, with cement floors and excellent drainage arrangements. The association was organized five years ago, and then represented 500 cows. Each member paid $2.70 per cow entered by him, which made a total capital of $1,350. The cost of the plant was $6,588. The balance of $5,292 was borrowed at 4 per cent interest, with notes for $540 falling due each year until all was paid. Each member was responsible for the debt in proportion to the number of cows entered. At she time of my visit there were 214 members, representing 700 cows. They were paid, as in other cases, the maximum price of a pound of butter for 28 pounds of milk. The organization differed from those already described in that the farmers were not compelled to take back the skim milk and buttermilk, but those who wanted it got what they required at about one-fourth of a cent per pound. The skim milk not sold was made into cheese at the creamery. They received at the time of my visit about 10,000 pounds of milk daily, in round numbers. The milk was raised to a temperature of 86° F. by running through a "forewarmer" before it ran into the separator. The cream was cooled with ice water as soon as separated, and about noon the prepared ferment was added, and by 6 a. m. the following day it was ready to churn. It was churned at 56° F., and butter usually came in thirty-five minutes. The superintendent worked the butter the first time by hand, after which it was laid away to cool for two hours; it was then worked on the butter-worker, 4 per cent of salt added, and immediately packed in barrels for shipment. It was kept in cold storage while in the creamery and sold once a week. Mr. Rasmussen prepared his own ferment from hand-skimmed milk in exactly the same manner as described for the Kildevæld, creamery. The skim milk was sterilized at 185° F. From the sterilizing apparatus it ran into a large vat, from which the orders from the farmers were filled, and what remained was made into skim-milk cheese, of which they made about 170 pounds daily. It required 16 pounds of milk to make a pound of cheese.

The milk was warmed and the rennet added in the manner already described. The cheese remained in the press for twenty-four hours. It was then put in strong brine for twenty-four hours and next put in the cheese-room, where it was daily wiped and turned for a month, and when the rind began to harden it was washed daily with brine. Their cheese sold, wholesale, for 4½ cents per pound avoirdupois. Patrons of the creamery had the privilege of buying cheese and butter at a trifle lower price than that asked in the market. The establishment was equipped with a seven horse-power boiler, a five horse power engine, a DeLaval "Alpha" separator, with the necessary line of tanks, cream barrels, buckets, etc., and also a line of cheese-making utensils. The superintendent in this creamery received about $272 per year as salary, with house, fuel, light, and dairy products, and 25 per cent of the receipts for butter above the top quotation by the exchange in Copenhagen. Out of this he paid and boarded his help, of which there were four persons: first, a chief dairywoman who got $67.50 per year and board; second, a young man who got $59.40 a year and board; third, a young man who got $33.75 per year and board, and, lastly, a dairy pupil, a young woman, who got $16.20 per year and board.

SNÓDE AND STOELSE COÖPERATIVE CREAMERY.

The superintendent of this creamery, Mr. P. Andersen, kindly furnished me with the following information: Eight thousand one hundred dollars was invested in the plant. Of this sum the building site cost $378, the building $2,970, machinery $2,970, and furniture and all other dairy utensils, with some other further improvements, some $1,782. All of this was borrowed money, on which interest was paid at the rate of 4 per cent per annum. Five thousand four hundred dollars were to be paid back in ten years, at the rate of $540 a year, and the remainder was to stand indefinitely. The association contained only 123 members, who had entered 650 cows. At that time the receipt of milk amounted to only 6,000 pounds daily, but in summer time this was more than doubled. From this was made an average of 210 pounds of butter daily, which in summer arose to 550 pounds. The members were paid, as in other places, the highest price per pound of butter for 28 pounds of milk; but they possessed a good class of cows, and it required only 26.6 pounds of milk to make a pound of butter. Fjord's control apparatus was used to test the milk, and all the milk was tested at least twice a week. It was not compulsory on the members to take back the skim milk and buttermilk, but it was sold to those who wanted it at about one-fourth of a cent per pound for buttermilk and one-third of a cent per pound for skim milk. All the skim milk not disposed of in this manner was made into cheese. That little creamery produced annually 121,000 pounds of cheese, or at an average rate of about 330 pounds daily. The cream was not sterilized because it was not found necessary. The strictest precautions to maintain absolute cleanliness were taken at every step, and they never had any cause to sterilize the cream. In winter the churning temperature was at about 60° F.; in summer it was somewhat lower. The churn was of the usual pattern, the dasher making 150 revolutions per minute. When granules began to show in the churn it was washed down with a few quarts of water of the same temperature as the cream. The butter was worked as soon as taken out of the churn for the removal of the buttermilk, and 4 per cent of salt added at once. One hour later it received a second working. It was then placed in a cooling-box, and in winter a third working was given it in two hours from the last, but in summer it remained in the cooler until the next morning, when it received the final working and was packed. Superintendent Andersen did not find it necessary to use any butter color. In fact, there are many places where none is used, and only little is added where color is used at all.

There being so much cheese manufactured, I obtained details in regard to the method followed. The skim milk was warmed to 85° F. and 14 per cent buttermilk was added and stirred violently and rennet added. It then stood for thirty minutes, when the curd was cut and stirred slowly, and at the same time the temperature was raised to 90° F. by injecting steam under the vat. When the whey was clear it was drawn off, and three-tenths of a pound of salt was added to the curd for every 100 pounds of milk, and worked in by hand. It was next put in the cheese cups and a light pressure applied. At the end of an hour it was taken out and turned and replaced under the press. Ten hours later it was turned again, and the following morning it was taken out and put in brine, where it remained for twenty-four hours. From the brine it was put into the cheese room, which was so arranged that it could be heated at pleasure by the waste steam from the engine. It was first placed near the steam pipes where there was a temperature of about 77° F. in winter; here it remained four days, being daily turned and wiped. After that it was gradually moved into a cooler temperature, remaining, however, in the cheese room for three months. If stored after that it was kept at a temperature of 55° F. The price received varied considerably with the market, the maximum being about 6¼ cents per pound avoirdupois. The whey was sold to farmers at about one-twelfth of a cent per pound.

NONNEBJERG FÆLLES CREAMERY.

This creamery is, in several respects, the most interesting commercial creamery I visited. It is located at the city of Skanderborg, and is owned and operated by a noted bacteriologist, Mr. E. A. Quist, who, in his laboratory connected with the creamery, prepares the pure cultures which I have already had occasion to mention. By the courtesy of Mr. Quist I was permitted to look into the details of his business. The plant consisted of a large and very substantial brick building (Fig. 28), the cost of which is immaterial, since it also contained a laboratory and other compartments not essential to a creamery. Mr. Quist bought the milk from about 1,500 cows, but at the time of my visit

FIG. 28.—Projection of one side of Quist's creamery building.

the supply amounted to only 10,000 pounds daily. He had built and equipped this creamery chiefly to afford him opportunities for testing his pure cultures, and as he was compelled to pay a high price for the milk the profit was not great. However, the equipment of the creamery and the management of the product reached the highest point of modern skill attainable under the conditions there presented.

The sweet milk was sterilized as soon as received, at a temperature of 167° F. It ran directly from the sterilizing apparatus into the separators. Mr. Quist had tested the effect of separating at different temperatures, and he found that the milk was skimmed cleaner when run through the separator at about 167° F. than it was when separated at any lower temperature. He would under no circumstances separate at a lower temperature than 95° F. He found that at 167° F. there remained fifteen one-hundredths of 1 per cent of fat in the milk; at 95° F. there remained nineteen one-hundredths of 1 per cent, but at 77° F.

analysis showed that there remained twenty-two one-hundredths of 1 per cent of fat in the milk; and he maintained that, aside from the fact that the milk was sterilized, it was economy to raise it to that temperature in order to skim it cleaner. He used two Burmeister & Waiue separators, as he maintained that they had advantages over others. They can raise the skim milk and cream to a height of 8 feet through pipes which can be directed to any part of the creamery, and much work in handling milk and cream is thus saved. Again, the latest pattern of this separator, which I saw in use there, was provided with a lid which could be closed perfectly air-tight. There is, however, a suction of air into the bowl when the machine is running; this air was admitted through a tube filled with sterilized cotton, which thus, as it were, strained the air before it came into contact with the milk and cream. Both milk and cream were run from the separators directly to coolers. In this case Smith's round cooler was used, which lowered the temperature to 46° F. These coolers were provided with a cap, or sort of lid made of tin, which fitted closely, and was designed to exclude the air as much as possible while the cream was trickling slowly down the sides. The notion that the coolers served any good purpose by aërating the milk is a mistaken one. It would be much better if the air were excluded, as the milk or cream becomes impregnated with bacteria from the air when thus exposed in a thin sheet over the sides of the cooler. The sole object in cooling the milk is to thus reduce the temperature so that the bacteria will cease to grow, and not, as is sometimes advocated, to expose the milk to the air, which has no effect on the creaming quality of the milk. When all the milk for the day had been separated Mr. Quist warmed a portion of the cream to 160° F., and this was mixed with the bulk of the cream in order to raise it all to a temperature of 68° F., and at this temperature he added 12 per cent of his pure culture. Cream thus prepared stood from 1 p. m. till 7:30 a. m. the next day, when it was ready to churn. The pure culture was used every day if the milk was not sterilized, as was sometimes the case; but when the milk was sterilized daily he used pure culture only once a week and buttermilk the rest of the time. When the milk was sterilized it was found that the cream required nearly twice the amount of pure culture in order to cause the proper degree of fermentation in the desired time than was needed when not sterilized. Sterilized cream, on the other hand, did not require such close watching. If kept at a given temperature it would always attain a given degree of acidity in the allotted time, and the souring could also be permitted to go further without injurious effects.

The churns were of the usual pattern of the country. The churning temperature varied with the season. At the time of my visit it was 57° F., but in summer it frequently went as low as 52° F. The butter was dipped out of the churn with a sieve, placed on the butter-worker, the buttermilk pressed out, and immediately afterward it was weighed and 5 per cent of salt added, thus giving it two workings at once. The third working took place three or four hours later in the winter, the butter being kept in a cooling box in the meantime; but in the summer it was not worked the last time until the next morning, being kept in the cooler all the time. Immediately after the last working it was packed in barrels of the usual size and placed in the storeroom to await shipment. Mr. Quist was particular to stop the churn at the right moment, not only for the sake of the consistency of the butter, but he maintained that if it was churned too long, or churned at too warm a temperature, the butter would contain a greater per cent of water than otherwise, and this affected its quality. The skim milk from this creamery was, for the most part, sold to people in the city, and that not disposed of in this manner was fed to swine.

I note the following points in regard to this creamery: (1) It was a solid brick structure which might last for centuries; (2) the ventilation was perfect; air could be admitted from all sides and the warm air could be let out by means of the ventilator in the roof; (3) it was constructed on the "gravity" plan; milk and cream could run directly to any desired place without having to be transported in buckets, thus saving a large amount of labor; (4) the floors were of natural Trinidad asphalt, and aside from being durable they could be kept scrupulously clean, and the drainage arrangements were perfect. I could not help comparing this to the wooden floors in our American creameries full of cracks and crevices, in which bacteria breed to perfection and through which not unfrequently bad odors arise from the water-soaked ground below.

The machinery and utensils had cost the owner the sum of $3,240. I enumerate the following:

(1) An eight horse-power boiler.
(2) A six horse-power engine.
(3) Two "B & W" separators, each with a capacity of 2,800 Danish pounds per hour.
(4) A receiving weight, on which rested a balanced weighing can, with a capacity of several hundred pounds. When the desired amount of milk had been weighed a light touch tilted this can so that the milk was discharged into—
(5) The receiving tank. A large, square can of heavy tin.
(6) A "forewarmer" or sterilizing apparatus, where the milk was heated to the desired temperature.
(7) The separators, which raise the cream through brass pipes to a little tin pan suspended from above, from which it runs through—
(8) Smith's cooler, which, in turn discharges into barrels.
(9) The skim milk is in like manner raised to a small tank above, directly from the separators, from which it runs to the delivery tank or through the sterilizer, as may be desired.
(10) A pump forced the water used in the coolers in a circle from a reservoir, filled with ice above the cooler, through the cooler and back again to the reservoir. This arrangement made it possible to save a good deal of ice, since the same ice water was used over and over again.
(11) The same pump was also used to convey buttermilk from the churns through a hose to a tank in the delivery room, where it was weighed out to customers.

(12) Two Smith's coolers, which have been described elsewhere.
(13) Two cream barrels, double, a tin can being fitted in an oaken casing.
(14) Two churns, also of oak wood.
(15) A large revolving butter-worker, of the American pattern, but which was highest in the center, so that the fluid as it was pressed out ran to the circumference.
(16) An oak-wood butter trough, serving more especially as a table.
(17) Two butter-coolers, of the pattern described and illustrated under Dairy Implements.

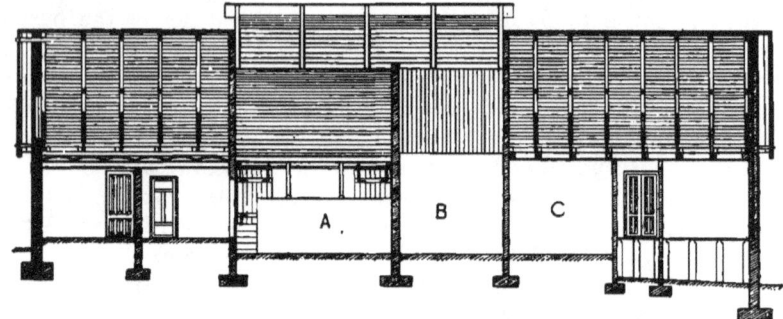

FIG. 29.—Vertical section from end of Quist's creamery building.

(18) A butter weight, on which the butter is weighed after the first working, in order to ascertain the required amount of salt.
(19) In a separate room cement basins for ice water in which to cool milk when this is desirable.
(20) A large cheese vat with copper bottom.
(21) Cheese presses.
(22) In wash room a hot-water tank, from which the necessary amount of hot water could be had at all times, when the engine was running.
(23) In the same place a steam jet, with arrangement for sterilizing all milk cans and other utensils.

I give herewith further illustrations of Mr. Quist's creamery. Fig. 29 shows a vertical section, from end to end, of the creamery. *A* is the

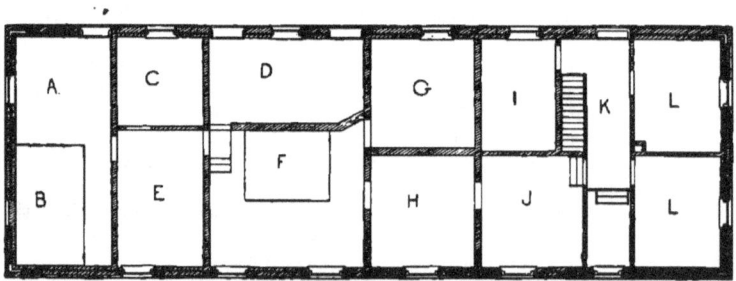

FIG. 30.—Plan of Quist's creamery building.

raised platform on which the milk is received and weighed and from which it runs down to the separator, *B* is the churning room, and *C* the room in which the butter is worked. The ventilator over the work room is a noticeable feature. This ventilator could be closed or opened at pleasure. Fig. 30 is the plan of the building. *A* is the coal room, *B* the boiler room, *C* the cheese room. This room could be warmed by steam from the boiler. *E* the engine room, *D* the platform on which were the milk vats, *F* the separating room below this platform, *G* the wash room, *H* the churning room, *I* office, *J* the room in which the butter was worked and cooled, *K* hall, and *LL* laboratories. There were rooms above the laboratories for the accommodation of the help.

To these descriptions I could add much more material of the same nature, but I trust that the methods described in the foregoing cases will enable creamery and dairy men to get a reasonably clear idea of the practice in the Danish dairies.

DAIRY BACTERIOLOGY.

It is only between two and three years since the use of pure cultures of bacteria were introduced into the creameries of Denmark, as a means of improving the butter, but the results have been so uniformly successful that they are now used in all dairies whenever there is necessity for them. The honor of the introduction of this improvement in creamery methods does not belong to any one man, though, perhaps Prof. V. Storch, director of the experimental laboratory at Copenhagen, deserves the "lion's share" of the credit. He has been at work on the problem for some six or eight years, and from time to time has published the results of his researches. Other bacteriologists took up the same line of work, and the result was that pure cultures of the beneficial bacteria were put upon the market by the three different laboratories at about the same time. Prof. Storch had already then isolated and cultivated several forms of these bacteria, but he has not put any of them on the market.

As the several investigators worked independently of each other, each can be credited with an original discovery, especially since the bacteria employed are not the same in all cases. From the investigations by Prof. Storch, Prof. Fjord, and others, it soon became evident that the quality of the butter depended, at least in a large degree, on the presence or absence of certain minute organisms. It was found that in faulty butter certain forms were present which, when isolated and cultivated, produced the characteristics which were objectionable. In like manner it was found that in high-class butter certain other forms were present, which would, in like manner, produce the characteristic aroma and flavor when cultivated by themselves. This led to the natural recognition of two general classes of bacteria, one of which was injurious to the interests of the dairy, and the other one beneficial. When this fact had been settled, the practical question before the investigators was how it would be possible to repress one class and encourage the other. Prof. Fjord had, in the meantime, perfected his pasteurizing apparatus, which has been figured and described elsewhere. This was invented chiefly with a view to improve the keeping qualities of skim milk so that it might reach the patrons and other consumers in a fresh and sweet condition. This was accomplished by heating it to a temperature of upwards of 150° F. It was found that this temperature destroyed enough of the bacteria which caused the milk to change to make it possible to keep it sweet for from twelve to twenty-four hours longer than when it is not thus heated. The next step was to apply the same treatment to the cream, or to the sweet milk before it was separated, with the same results. Heated to a temperature of between 150° and 160° F., or upwards, it was found that the most active forms of the bacteria were killed, and that by again cooling the cream to about 75° or 80° F., at which bacterial life becomes active, the cream could be inoculated by any desirable form of bacteria if these could be obtained from pure cultures, and that the forms with which the cream was thus impregnated, meeting with no opposition from other forms, would develop rapidly in enormous numbers and give their peculiar characteristics to the butter. This is exactly what is now done in practice. The cream is not always pasteurized because, if there are no injurious bacteria present, at least in such numbers as to cause a deterioration of the product, there is no necessity for attempting to kill them, and the addition in sufficient quantity of a pure culture would at once give the latter the upper hand, and their peculiarities would become prominent. A rather more thorough sterilization would be effected if the milk were raised to the boiling point; but a temperature of much over 160° F. gives the characteristic boiled taste to both milk and cream, which is objectionable and must be avoided. It is found in practice that this temperature destroys nearly all the organisms in active growth. The spores will survive this temperature, but it takes them longer to develop and by the time they become ready the pure culture has the mastery.

As a higher degree of heat than that required for their normal development is destructive to the bacteria, so in like manner a reduction of the temperature retards their growth. It does not destroy them, if not below the freezing point, but it stops their development and renders them inactive. It is for this reason that pains should always be taken to reduce the temperature of the milk, by means of ice water, to a point as near the freezing point as practicable. Heat and cold, relatively speaking, are therefore effective means in controlling bacterial life in the creamery.

There were at the time of my visit three laboratories in which pure cultures were propagated and sold to the dairies. One of these was the laboratory of Christian Hansen, the famous butter color and rennet manufacturer, whose products are well known in this country. Another was a firm of chemists named Blauenfeldt & Tvede. Both of these laboratories were in Copenhagen. A third laboratory belonged to Mr. E. A. Quist, of Skanderborg, whom I have already had occasion to mention in the description of his creamery. These dealers in the pure cultures keep their methods of propagation secret. The isolation of the germs can, of course, be accomplished by any bacteriologist; but they claim that it is only through a long series of experiments that they have hit upon a composition for the nutritive fluid in which to grow them to best advantage. It also requires certain forms of apparatus to which they may lay claim as inventors, and these features they do not propose to divulge, as it would probably increase competition to a point beyond profitable production. Moreover, I was informed that each form of these minute organisms had to be treated in a manner peculiar to itself, and as the several growers did not deal in the same bacterial forms, their methods of treatment in the laboratory were not alike. How many forms of the beneficial bacteria are in existence is at present unknown; but it is known that they are numerous. A dozen or more forms have already been discovered. Blauenfeldt & Tvede informed me that their culture contained many forms, but how many was not stated.

Mr. Quist, on the other hand, uses only two forms, which I had opportunity to study through the microscope. There was a decided difference in the smell and taste of the preparations offered by the two firms. Blauenfeldt & Tvede's cultures had a sharp, sour taste and smell. Mr. Quist's cultures were less acid and possessed a peculiar nutty aroma, such as we find in the best samples of butter. I have had opportunity to see the effect of Mr. Quist's culture in this country. I bought samples of him which he shipped to the Department of Agriculture. A portion of these samples was forwarded to me, and I tried them in the Belle Springs creamery, owned by Mr. J. E. Nissley, the president of the Kansas Dairymen's Association.

The cream was not sterilized before the cultures were added, but they had a decided influence on the butter. Both Mr. Nissley and his butter-maker pronounced the quality superior to any they had made formerly, and they at once became converts to the process. I forwarded samples of the pure cultures to Prof. H. C. Wallace, who has charge of the dairying in the Iowa State Agricultural College, but I have at this writing not heard with what results they were used. In Denmark, where the cultures will be in transit at most only a couple of days before they reach their destination on the dairy farms, they are put up in a preparation of skim milk; but in shipping to this country, where they may be in transit for many weeks, they must be specially prepared in order to retain their activity the necessary length of time. The samples shipped by Mr. Quist were sent in three mediums; one a preparation of milk sugar; another in sterilized cotton, and the third in a nutritive fluid of his own invention. At the Belle Springs creamery we used only the first and the last of these. Although they had been in transit from the 10th of March until the 5th of June, they appeared to be perfectly fresh and ready for business. The cotton preparation I did not try. Should any of our creamery men decide to try Mr. Quist's cultures, they can be had without fear of deterioration on the journey. It is, however, to be supposed that our bacteriologists will soon take this matter in hand and give us pure cultures within easy reach of the creameries in this country. The American branch of Christian Hansen's laboratory prepares and sells the pure cultures, which had their origin in his laboratory at Copenhagen.

CONSTRUCTION OF ICE HOUSES.

Ice being used so largely in the Danish dairies, they have given considerable attention to the construction of ice houses. Formerly it was customary to store the ice in a pit in the ground, this pit being dug on a hill or rising ground, so that a drain could be laid from the bottom of it to carry the water off readily. These pits were walled up with brick or granite and covered with thatch. But it was found that this construction was neither convenient nor economical, and it has long since been abandoned. Their ice houses are now constructed above ground, and, whenever practicable, in direct connection with the creamery. Although ice is not a scarce article in that country, it has been found more economical to build a substantial ice house with double walls

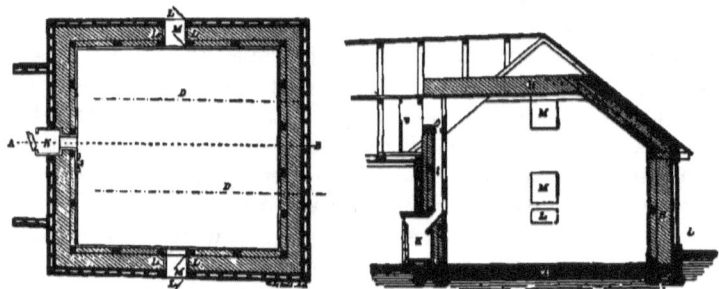

FIG. 31.—Ground plan and section of ice house.

than to put the ice in a flimsy structure with thin walls, through which the changes of temperature are readily felt.

Fig. 31 shows the plan and section of an ice house of modern construction, built in connection with a creamery. Both the outside and inside walls are, in this case, of wood, but they are also frequently built of brick. The plan shows that the outside studding is boarded up on both sides. On the outside, ordinary weather-boarding is used, but on the inside it should be made as tight as possible. Inside of this shell, and 2 feet from it all around, is another set of studding which is also boarded up on both sides, the boards being fitted nicely together. The 2-foot space between these two walls is filled with some non-heat-conducting material, chaffed straw or hay being the most common. Any material thus used will, in the course of two or three years, have gathered moisture so that it will begin to mold, or, if it is of a nature which prevents its molding, it will nevertheless be moist, and in this condition it has partly lost its non-conducting properties and it ought to be renewed. It is therefore essential to have small doors at convenient places in the outside shell, near the ground, through which the packing can be removed, and others near the top through which it can be renewed. The space is large enough to admit a person to tramp it together.

The ice house here represented opens into the creamery and, in this case, no special anteroom is therefore needed; but if the entrance is from the outside an anteroom is essential in order that the warm air may be excluded from the ice house on entering. In the section of this ice house the letters $H H$ represent the chaff which is packed in between the double walls. $M M$ are doors through which the ice house is to be filled and $L L$ are doors used for the renewal of the chaff. The letter T represents a layer of peat on which the ice rests. It will be noticed that the layer of chaff extends over the ice as well as up the sides of the building. The ice is removed through the shute t and falls into the box K, from which it is removed as wanted during the day. Entrance to this ice house is gained at V, under the ceiling, where there also is a window to admit some light. In the plan the letters L and M represent the openings, the same as in the section. K is the box into which the ice is thrown, $D D$ are drains which carry off the water as the ice melts and the line $A B$ represents the point at which the section is drawn.

In this connection it is interesting to note an experiment carried out by Prof. Fjord to ascertain the efficiency of the substances named as packing materials to be used between the walls of ice houses. The results are based upon the amount of water obtained from melting ice kept in an ice box, placed in a warm room, and the double walls of which were successively filled with the materials named. Chaffed straw is taken as the standard and represents 100. The figures are as follows:

Chaffed straw	air dry..	100	Wheat straw	air dry..	110
Cotton	do...	79	Peat dust	do...	116
Barley hulls	do...	90	Sawdust	green..	170
Wheat chaff	do...	92	Peat	damp..	260
Oat chaff	do...	94	Sawdust	wet..	260
Dry leaves	do...	96	Earth	do...	560
Rice hulls	do...	101	Sand	do...	630
Buckwheat hulls	do...	104			

The proper use of ice in storerooms is also an important point. In connection with the experimental laboratory in Copenhagen is an exhibition building for dairy products. It is in this building that the frequent competitive exhibitions of butter from dairies all over the country are held. It is essential that the butter should be kept at a low temperature, and to this end Prof. Fjord constructed an ice house in connection with it which is so arranged that the air which enters the storeroom must pass over the ice in the ice house. There are ventilators placed near the bottom of the wall which separates the ice house from the storeroom, and the cold air from the ice house flows through these into the storeroom. The principle is illustrated in Fig. 32, the arrows showing the course of the air currents. The cold air comes out from the ice directly under the butter packages, and as it becomes warmer it rises and again enters the ice house, or large ice box, as the case may be, at the top. It is a principle which it may be advantageous for our creameries to put into practice.

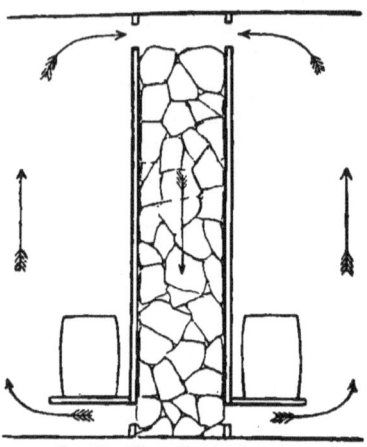

FIG. 32.—Use of ice in storeroom.

STATE AID TO THE DAIRY INDUSTRY.

As I have shown in the early portion of this report, dairying is the chief industry in Denmark, and it would manifestly be to the interest of the state to aid in its development in every possible way. The persons with whom I conversed on the subject were, as a rule, of the opinion that the state did not do its full duty in this respect. However, considering that it is a small country, under heavy expenses in maintaining the Government, and with but limited resources, the state has given no inconsiderable aid in this direction. It does not expend large sums in any one direction. Its policy is, on the other hand, to encourage the people by small money donations, and, by furnishing them expert assistants, to solve for themselves the problems as they appear. The experimental laboratory at Copenhagen should perhaps be named first. It is maintained wholly by the state in the interest of the industries among which dairying, of course, takes the leading position. It was in the capacity of director of this laboratory that Prof. Fjord and his many able assistants made the long series of experiments and investigations into the various phases of the dairy industry which have been so fruitful in beneficial results. Yet these investigations were made without any great cost to the state. As a rule, the large farmers throughout the country, who were interested in the results, lent their herds to these experiments with unstinted hand, free of charge. Under these conditions Prof. Fjord was able to carry on experiments at several—frequently at as many as half a dozen—farms at once. He furnished the expert assistants, who had direct charge of the experiments and supervised the work, while the farmer, who owned the place where the work was carried on, as a rule paid for the labor.

The Government aids indirectly by offering premiums for the best dairy cattle at the shows. Such premiums are not, however, restricted to the dairy interest, but have in view the improvement of domestic animals of all kinds. It encourages the improvement of the dairy breeds by aiding the "bull associations," to which I have already had occasion to refer. For this purpose $13,500 are at present divided yearly among the associations in various parts of the country. Thus, the state will pay one-third of the cost of keeping these bulls, within the limits of the sum named, provided the association conforms to specified rules. And, in order to be entitled to this aid the bull must be at least two years old, he must not be put to more than 100 cows, and he must be of approved quality and pure breed.

The state gives direct aid to a limited number of young men and women who desire to become experts in the dairy business. They will thus be sent to some approved agricultural school for a time, and later to some practical dairy of more or less renown, where they can obtain the necessary information and experience. Twenty-two pupils received state aid of this character in 1892 at a cost of only about $1,620.

The state aids indirectly in the advancement of the dairy industry through the Royal Agricultural Society, which is supported in part by the state. This society has been of untold benefit to Danish agriculture. It was organized in 1769, and has ever since labored by the most effective means within its reach to improve agriculture and the condition of the farmer. Its membership has, as a rule, at all times been drawn from the leading men of the country, and these have contributed freely both of their substance and work to further the object for which the society was organized. Their most effective means are, perhaps, the education in agriculture of promising young men who, in turn, become leaders in the industry and influential factors in its improvement. This has been the main line of work for many years and is still continued. The society also maintains at least one expert adviser in dairying, whose counsel is available to any one who stands in need of advice. This post is at present filled by Mr. Bernhard Bóggild, who is not only a scientist but an expert in all dairy matters and an authority everywhere recognized. He is author of the book on dairying I have already mentioned, which is, perhaps, the best work on the subject in print. The society also aids in the improvement of the dairy cattle by supplementing the Government in giving prizes at shows and in aiding in the purchase of good bulls to be used by the bull associations. It aids by giving publicity to all useful information in the form of pamphlets and reports, which otherwise would not reach any considerable number of the farmers. The Royal Agricultural

Society of Denmark must thus be considered as affording important aid to the dairy industry, in which work it is assisted and encouraged by the state.

The state aids the dairy by maintaining three dairy experts as advisers to the people. Each one of these is assigned a definite territory. They are all under the direction of the minister of the interior. In all there are nine such advisers for the benefit of agriculture, but three of them have their work confined to the dairy. These gentlemen may be called by any creamery or dairyman in the district to assist in discovering faults in the butter, to give their advice in regard to methods of treatment of the cattle, and of the milk and butter, and, in short, to render every assistance in their power in aiding the dairy industry. For this service the adviser is paid by the state; but the person calling him pays a certain proportion of the traveling expenses and maintains him with board and lodging while at his place. I can perhaps give no better idea of the nature of this work than by quoting a portion of the report of one of them to the minister of the interior for the year 1891. This report is by Stats-Konsulent (State Adviser) J. Nissen-Dall, who is located in the city of Fredericia, and whose activity is confined to a portion of the southern peninsula and several of the smaller islands. He says:

I have during the time covered by this report been called upon to give assistance in the dairies of my district one hundred and forty-five times. I have given twenty-seven lectures on dairy matters. I have, by invitation, attended eight meetings of the farmers, and I have acted as judge of dairy exhibits nineteen times, most of the exhibitions being held at the experimental laboratory. I attended an exhibition of cheese at the same laboratory, and I attended three exhibitions of butter under the auspices of the dairymen's association. In conjunction with Konsulenterne (advisers) Bóggild, Segelcke, and Buhl—all dairy advisers—I have visited three dairies on Funen to witness experiments in pasteurizing milk and cream. Further, I have, with pecuniary assistance from the Royal Danish Agricultural Society, visited a number of dairies where the pasteurizing of cream was being introduced, and I also made investigations in the neighborhood of Vejle. Toward the close of July, 1891, I was present at the final examination of the pupils in the Ribe Dairy School. In connection with the exhibition of butter, to be held in Góteborg (Sweden), I visited seven dairies in my district during May and June. I attended the exhibition in Góteborg, from the 3d to the 9th of August. Besides all of this I have answered a large number of questions by mail. The majority of my lectures have been held in the interest of coöperative creameries, where my subjec has been The Production and Treatment of the Milk. I lectured once before the members of the Fodder Stuff Association, and once at an exhibition of cheese in Ringe.

This will give a fair idea of the nature of the work assigned to these advisers, and the results prove that the plan is thoroughly practical. This business of advising in dairy matters has become a profession in Denmark. Besides the four official advisers, one maintained by the agricultural society and three by the state, very many of the dairy associations, of which there are many throughout the country, maintain advisers of their own, and whenever a fault appears in the dairy or creamery which the man in charge is unable to remedy an adviser is called in to investigate the cause and remedy the fault, just as a farmer here will call a veterinarian when his horse or cow gets sick, or a doctor when a member of his family gets sick. In dairies where hundreds of pounds of butter are made daily and where a deterioration in quality is sure to be followed by a decrease in price, it is of the utmost importance to remedy a defect as soon as it appears, and this is the business of the adviser.

MARKETS FOR DANISH DAIRY PRODUCTS.

Statistics published by the Government for the year 1891 show that butter was exported from Denmark to the following countries during that year, to the amounts named:

	Danish pounds.	Pounds avoirdupois.
Faroe Islands	17,543	19,297
Iceland	15,293	16,822
Greenland	13,618	14,980
Danish Possessions in West Indies	1,314	1,445
Norway	202,730	223,003
Sweden	482,950	531,245
Russia	623	685
To Hamburg	203,425	223,767
Lubeck	348,350	383,185
Sleavig-Holstein and Lauenburg	860,474	946,521
To the rest of Germany	10,240	11,264
To England	88,959,471	97,855,418
Holland	155,953	171,548
Belgium	52,726	57,998
France	1,211	1,332
Portugal	2,803	3,083
Spain	18,952	20,847
Italy	94,526	103,978
United States	5,500	6,050
To miscellaneous places	7,560	8,316
Total	91,435,262	100,602,784

ENGLISH IMPORTS OF DANISH BUTTER.

England, it will be noticed, is the only country which consumes Danish butter in any considerable quantity, and this is the market which they cultivate above all others. I stopped in London a few days in order to investigate this subject on the spot, and spent considerable time among the importers of Danish butter. What I learned in this regard I stated briefly in my preliminary report, and I can not do better now than to repeat what I then said, which was as follows:

All the testimony I gathered agrees in this, that the Danish butter brings the top price in the English market with one exception, and that exception is made in favor of the comparatively small amount of fresh unsalted butter shipped to London from northern France. It caters to the taste of a small but select class of consumers, and it reaches their tables inside of twelve hours from the churn. This butter, I was told, brings from one to three or four pence more per pound than the Danish butter. I tasted this butter, and to me it lacked flavor and the pleasant briskness peculiar to a fine grade of salted butter, but there is no accounting for tastes. There is a market for such butter in London, and the dairymen from northern France supply it. The Danes have tried to supply it, but their product can not reach England in less than three days, and this length of time was fatal to the rich, creamy flavor which the market demanded, and the attempt was given up.

I found also that the Danish butter finds its best market in the manufacturing towns, and that these consume relatively much more of it than the capital. This would indicate that it goes especially to the middle class and well-to-do artisans.

I inquired particularly about the manner of shipment and whether any attempt was made to keep it in a uniform temperature during transit, and I found that so far the temperature had not been controlled. It had been tried and proved that nothing was gained by it. The conditions are such that it must be handled several times, and often many times, between the dairy and its destination. It must be transferred from wagon to railway, and from railway to boat, several times, following the route of transportation from island to island to the port of shipment, and during these transfers it is often exposed for hours to a burning heat or chilling cold, which would so far affect it that no attempt to equalize the temperature where it could be controlled could remedy the damage it might already have received, while it stood in the sun on the wharf or railroad station. It is true only a very small per cent is injured from these causes, but the risk still exists. Transportation which shall be absolutely safe to the texture and flavor of the Danish butter is still an unsolved problem. Nearly all Danish butter is packed and shipped to England in small barrels, of which there are two sizes, holding, respectively, 56 and 112 pounds. This sort of package is easily handled and has become customary. The Australian and New Zealand butter is usually shipped in square boxes, holding almost 36 pounds. The French butter above mentioned is done up in 2-pound rolls and forwarded in baskets containing usually 24 pounds. To my surprise I found in several of the warehouses considerable quantities of Russian butter. Russia began to ship butter to England five or six years ago, and the amount is growing year by year. It is put up in barrels in imitation of the Danish butter.

The Danish butter maintains its high standing chiefly through its uniformity. I sampled numerous packages from various parts of the country and found them very nearly all alike. It is all first class; it all has the same bright straw color, and the same degree of saltness, and it varies but very slightly in aroma, flavor, and texture. Mr. Jacobsen told me that he had endeavored to secure consignments of a cheaper grade of butter, as he thought he had a market for it, but word came back that it could not be found; no inferior butter was offered for export. This uniformity in quality inspires both dealer and consumer with confidence. They know they can buy the Danish butter and be sure of getting a good article without necessitating their tasting it before they purchase. Not so, I was told, with other countries. While they might forward some very fine butter, it was never safe to depend upon it.

As to the prices which wholesale dealers in London realize on Danish butter, they rule low from an American point of view. There are fluctuations, of course, but it sells generally from 14d to 18d a pound, the latter figure being considered high.

To give an idea of the growth of the Danish export butter to England in recent years, I quote the following figures from the "Annual statement of the trade of the United Kingdom," which I procured. It is an official and entirely reliable publication:

English imports of butter from Denmark.

	*Cwts.		*Cwts.
1887	487,536	1890	824,749
1888	604,422	1891	876,211
1889	677,398	1892	863,522

Value of same in pounds sterling.

1887	2,668,694	1890	4,422,257
1888	3,334,364	1891	4,865,842
1889	3,742,860	1892	4,848,735

*Cwts. = 112 pounds avoirdupois.

I can not comment on these figures now, but they speak for themselves. At the same time the import of butter from the following countries has also increased: Sweden, Russia, Belgium, France, United States, New South Wales, New Zealand, and Canada. The greatest increase has been made by New Zealand, but still the largest import therefrom was in 1891, and amounted to only 28,647 cwts. The imports of butter from Norway, Germany, and Holland have materially decreased in this time.

STATE AID TO FOREIGN MARKETS.

To aid in the sale of Danish agricultural products in the English market, the Government detailed an official in 1888 to be permanently located in England, whose duties were to aid by all means in his power in the sale of the Danish dairy products. The office is filled by an accomplished scientist, Mr. H. Faber, who has, according to the published records, done most excellent work in the line of his appointment. To give a more complete idea of the nature of his mission I translate the following instructions to him from the minister of the interior, as published in a report from the interior department for the years 1889 and 1890, entitled "Report of the Landókonomiske Konsulentvirksomhed:"

INSTRUCTIONS TO GOVERNMENT AGENT FABER.

(1) It will be your duty to support the good name and sale of Danish agricultural products, and particularly the dairy products on the English markets, by all the means at your disposal; and in so far as you find these means unsatisfactory, to make propositions for new and effective aids.

(2) You must direct your attention to the conditions governing trade and transportation of Danish agricultural products, and particularly the dairy products, both before they reach the English market and after they arrive there.

(3) It will be your duty to meet and correct through the press, and chiefly through the English press, all false and injurious statements concerning the Danish agriculture, and particularly our dairy industry and its products, and take the lead in setting a proper valuation on these.

(4) Your attention must be directed to frauds, both in and outside of England, which can injure the good name of Danish butter—as, for example, the misuse of Danish names, adulteration of Danish butter with oleomargarine, and the like—and make proposals for counteracting such frauds. For that purpose you must be supplied with the necessary apparatus, chemical and microscopical, to enable you to discover such adulterations.

(5) It will be your duty to keep your attention directed to the markets and ascertain if other and profitable markets can be opened for our agricultural and particularly our dairy products.

(6) When occasion demands it, and at least once a year, you must report through the Royal Danish Agricultural Society on the English market for our agricultural and especially for our dairy products, with such observations as you may see fit to make on the subject, particularly concerning the demands of the consumers, the faults and wants in our products, which should be corrected, and concerning such alterations in trade methods as may seem desirable.

(7) It will be your duty, as far as possible, to answer all inquiries directed to you, whether from Danish institutions or from men in private life concerning agriculture and the dairy. In like manner you ought to answer similar inquiries from trades-

men and consumers of Danish agricultural and dairy products in England, in so far as you may thereby serve Danish interests.

(8) You must neither directly nor indirectly allow yourself to become financially interested in the sale of Danish agricultural products or in other trade affairs.

In compliance with the above instructions, Mr. Faber took hold of his work with a vim. We learn from reports to his Government that he set about to correct false impressions concerning Danish dairying, through the press, exposed dealers who pretended to sell Danish butter, but in reality handled inferior articles from other countries. He even goes so far as to prosecute under English law those whom he can prove adulterate Danish butter or in other ways injure the trade in the genuine article. Comments are unnecessary. He renders signal service to the country in his appointed field of labor, and doubtless the increasing demand for Danish butter in England is due largely to his efforts.

RESTRICTIONS ON THE SALE OF OLEOMARGARINE.

In Denmark, as in the United States, the unrestricted sale of oleomargarine has proved to be injurious to the agricultural interests and especially to the dairy interests. To prevent this, strict laws have been enacted which regulate the manufacture and sale of this article. To quote the law, or even the chief points of it in this report, would perhaps be improper; but I will briefly note some of the leading features of the traffic and its restrictions. The law makes a distinction between "margarine" and "oleomargarine." It appears from statistics for the year, from the 1st of April, 1891, to the 1st of March, 1892, that there were in all sixteen factories where "margarine" was made and one where "oleomargarine" was made, which together produced 13,339,984 Danish pounds, for the period covered, and that there were in all 7,991 places in the country on the 31st of March, 1892, where this material was sold. This included both retail and wholesale houses. Among the chief points in the regulations concerning its sale are to be noted—

(1) The oleomargarine shall be colored light yellow. And as a standard of comparison color tables have been adopted in which different shades are numbered, the law providing that the color must not be darker than No. 9 of that scale, which is a very light straw yellow.

(2) That oleomargarine shall always be put in tubs or barrels, which must differ in shape from the ordinary packages in which butter is kept. The form adopted is an oval tub or barrel, in which the major axis shall be at least one and a half times longer than the minor axis, and the term "Margarine" shall be marked upon the ends and sides in very large letters. The accompanying illustration (Fig. 32) shows the form of the receptacle and the marking. This is not confined to large packages. All smaller vessels used to hold oleomargarine in the retail stores shall be of the same form and distinctly marked in the same manner, and all wrapping material used when purchases are wrapped up for customers shall be marked in the same manner; and, further, the per cent of butter in the mixture, if any, shall likewise be marked on the packages.

(3) All who deal in oleomargarine in any form shall procure a license from the Government before they can begin business.

(4) Three oleomargarine inspectors are appointed by the Government, each of whom has a definite district. These inspectors are charged with the duty of seeing that dealers and manufacturers comply with the law. They have authority to enter any establishment where butter is manufactured and sold and where oleomargarine is manufactured and sold, to examine the books and look into the details of the business, and they are required to take samples frequently, which are forwarded to a laboratory for analysis.

(5) The law prohibits the manufacture of butter and oleomargarine on the same premises.

These are only a few of the leading points, which, however, may serve to give an idea of the thoroughness of the control under which it is kept.

The penalties for violation of the law are severe and punishment is sure and swift. This law was first enacted in 1885, when, however, it was found to be too lenient. Later amendments have strengthened it

FIG, 33.—Required shape and marking of oleomargarine package (reduced one-half.)

on several points, and evasions of the law are now of comparatively rare occurrence, which is shown by the following statistics: From the 1st of May, 1888, to 31st of March, 1889, there were 176 convictions for violations of the law; from the 1st of April, 1889, to the 31st of March, 1890, there were 81 convictions; and from the 1st of April, 1890, to the 31st of March, 1891, there were but 36 convictions. The dairymen generally are satisfied with the workings of the law.

AGRICULTURAL AND DAIRY EDUCATION.

The two lines of education are so intimately connected that it is difficult to separate them from each other, and I therefore treat them together. There are a large number of agricultural schools and high schools in the country, nearly all of which give more are less instruction in dairy matters. I shall in the following account give a brief description of these schools, as far as I could ascertain the facts during the short time at my disposal. The institution which ranks above all others in the country is the "Royal Veterinary and Agricultural College" at Copenhagen. This is an old institution, having been in existence more than one hundred years. It was first begun as a veterinary school, and later branches in agriculture were added to it, but the veterinary branch of the institution continues to be an important one.

A law dated April 12, 1892, concerning the institution, of which I have obtained a copy, requires in its first paragraph the number of teachers in each branch to be as follows:

(1) In veterinary science, 3; (2) in agriculture, including dairying, 3; (3) in stock-breeding, 2; (4) in forestry, 2; (5) in surveying, 2; (6) in botany, 2; (7) in economic horticulture, 1; (8) in anatomy, 1; (9) in animal physiology, 1; (10) in chemistry, including agricultural chemistry, 2; (11) in physics, 1; (12) in zoölogy, 1.

This is exclusive of assistants and lecturers, for the employment of which the same law makes an appropriation of about $8,834.50 annually. The same law puts the salary of a professor at $864 a year, with an addition of $162 for every five years he remains in the college. This is a relatively much higher salary than is paid to the same class of teachers in this country. The same law appropriates $233,550 for the enlargement of the institution in nearly all of its branches, said amount to be expended in two years. In a report of the institution for 1891, which I obtained, I find the number of students given as 372. Provision is made for both long and short courses, so that it is difficult to say just what the length of the course is, but it does not exceed four years. The instruction is not free, but certain of the students are assisted by the state. Such assistance is invariably given to the best students. The dairy instruction is in charge of Prof. Segelcke, to whom I have already had occasion to refer. The teaching at the school is entirely theoretical, as far as the dairy instruction is concerned, but before a diploma is granted the student is required to spend a given time, which varies with his accomplishments, in a good dairy where the practical information can be fully supplied. The dairying is given as a part of the course in agriculture. I visited the institution and saw some of the students at work. The instruction is most thorough and confined strictly to agriculture and the related sciences. There is no literary instruction whatever given in the institution. This students are required to have before they enter.

Next to this institution comes a class of agricultural schools, some ten in number, all of which are private institutions. These, however, receive state aid in proportion to the number of students they have, the larger schools receiving each $810 annually. At all of these schools the students pay for their instruction. In most of them the course is two years in length and confined strictly to agriculture and the related sciences. Most of them give only theoretical instruction in dairying, the practice being obtained from some first-class dairy. I will briefly mention some of these schools.

(1) *Dalum Agricultural School, per Odense.*—This is the largest of that class of institutions. It had at the time of my visit to it 107 pupils, young men of the average age of 23 years, and from all parts of the country. The course was two years in length, thoroughly practical in its nature, and included as much of the sciences related to agriculture

as the time would permit. Dairy instruction was given during the summer months. I have already had occasion to mention the farm connected with this institution.

(2) *The Classenske Agricultural School, Næsgaard, on the Island of Falster.*—They have here but a limited number of pupils. The instruction is confined strictly to agriculture and dairying.

(3) *Lyngby Agricultural School, per Lyngby.*—There is an experiment station connected with this school maintained by the state.

(4) *Thune Agricultural School.*—This gives theoretical instruction only, and is designed to accommodate students who can spend only a short time in school. It has two courses, one of nine months and one of six months. It has 58 pupils.

(5) *Ladelund Agricultural School, per Brörub.*—This institution has some 70 students and it gives theoretical instruction in dairying, as well as in agriculture.

(6) *Malling Agricultural School.*—There are 40 students at this school. It is a well-equipped institution of high standing.

(7) *Yding Agricultural School, per Skanderborg.*

(8) *Morsó Agricultural School.*

(9) *Odense Agricultural School.*

(10) *Lyby Agricultural School.*

All of these are technical agricultural schools. But aside from them there are a large number of ordinary high schools which give agricultural instruction. It is estimated that there are about 100 of this class of institutions, many of which are most excellent. They are not classed with the agricultural schools because their main instruction is literary in its character. But, as stated, nearly all give some instruction in agriculture and dairying, and in the aggregate their influence is felt as a force in agricultural education.

Next to the schools comes the instruction received in the dairies. There are some 2,000 dairies in the country which receive pupils, and it is here that the majority of dairymen are educated. The instruction is of the most practical nature, the pupils doing any work which the business requires. As I have already had occasion to remark, these pupils usually receive their board and lodging and a very small salary besides, though in a few cases they pay for the privilege of working in the dairy. In some cases the dairy superintendent lectures to the pupils and thus, in a measure, supplies the lack of theoretical instruction, but this is the exception and not the rule.

o

www.ingramcontent.com/pod-product-compliance
Lightning Source LLC
Chambersburg PA
CBHW020105170426
43199CB00009B/396